100
BIKE RIDES
OF A LIFETIME

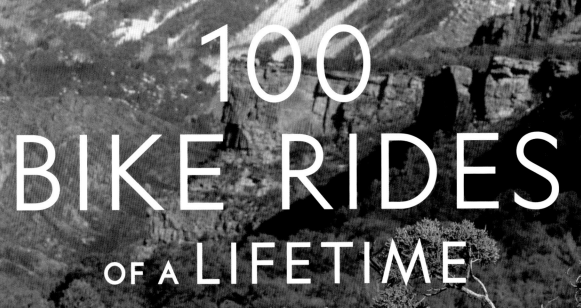

100 BIKE RIDES
OF A LIFETIME

*The World's Ultimate
Cycling Experiences*

ROFF SMITH

FOREWORD BY **KATE COURTNEY**

**NATIONAL
GEOGRAPHIC**

WASHINGTON, D.C.

CONTENTS

FOREWORD BY KATE COURTNEY 6

INTRODUCTION 8

PART ONE **THE AMERICAS** 10

PART TWO **EUROPE** 166

PART THREE **AFRICA, ASIA & OCEANIA** 302

RIDES BY COUNTRY 392

ACKNOWLEDGMENTS 395

ILLUSTRATIONS CREDITS 396

LEFT: Cyclists pass the storybook town of Blois, a UNESCO World Heritage site, in France's Loire Valley on the Loire à Vélo path (page 234).

PAGES 2-3: The Porcupine Rim Trail, part of the Whole Enchilada trail (page 42) outside Moab, Utah

FOREWORD

I was raised at the base of Mount Tamalpais in Marin County, California. From our backyard, the peak dominated the horizon. I grew up with my face pressed skyward, my gaze often resting on the summit, but it wasn't until I discovered mountain biking that I reached the top of Mount Tamalpais.

I have vivid memories of that day, sitting on the back of a tandem mountain bike as my dad led us up the mountain. We climbed the iconic Old Railroad Grade Trail with views stretching out in all directions. I remember how I felt when we reached the top, our house a tiny brown dot in the distance: I felt so very big and powerful, in awe of the fact that we had transported ourselves there. Yet I also felt so small—the world expanding out beneath me in all directions. It was magical. We stopped for blueberry pancakes on the way home, and I was hooked.

It feels like fate that I would become a professional mountain bike racer. Not only is Mount Tam (page 132) a beautiful place to ride, it is also famously where mountain biking was invented in the 1960s and '70s. Legends such as Tom Ritchey, Joe Breeze, Otis Guy, and Gary Fisher raced klunkers down the iconic Repack fire road (so named because riders had to "repack" their brakes at the bottom). But before I started racing, I didn't know any of this. I simply fell in love with being out on the mountain, with the feeling of pushing up to the summit and flying back down.

When I did begin racing, cycling became the home for my competitive spirit and the start of a new adventure. If those early days of mountain biking opened up my hometown to me, racing opened up the world. I have been lucky enough to ride so many of the trails and roads showcased in this beautiful book: taking on the Whole Enchilada in Utah (page 42), and tackling Passo di Gavia and climbing Stelvio in Italy (page 266). Through these experiences, cycling has become about more than time outside and blueberry pancakes, but in some ways, it is still marked by simple joys.

A bike ride can be anything. It can be a chance to explore a new place, to discover what lies around the next bend, or to reach the summit of the peak off in the distance. It can be a way to spend time with people you love. It can even be a vehicle that takes you to cookies and pancakes and post-ride beers. Most important, I firmly believe that cycling opens up experiences that change us for the better.

The first time I reached the summit of Mount Tamalpais, I left my parents' home and returned just a few hours later to the exact same place. Yet it completely changed my view of the world. I saw things I had not seen before and did something I hadn't known I could do. This is the joy of cycling and the value of adventure.

I hope that this book inspires you to embrace the magic of exploring by bike. Its pages are filled with iconic roads and trails that will lead you to some of the most beautiful places in the world. In *100 Bike Rides of a Lifetime,* you will find new peaks to look toward and adventures to plan.

—Kate Courtney, *U.S. Olympian and 2018 XCO World Champion*

Cyclist Kate Courtney
in her Team U.S.A. kit
for the 2020 Olympics
in Tokyo, Japan

INTRODUCTION

"When the spirits are low, when the day appears dark, when work becomes monotonous, when hope hardly seems worth having, just mount a bicycle and go out for a spin down the road, without thought on anything but the ride you are taking." — SIR ARTHUR CONAN DOYLE, 1896

There are few greater pleasures in life than going for a bike ride and feeling that old familiar sense of aerial liberation as you set off down the road, bound on an adventure of your own. But what makes a great ride? Ask mountain bikers and they'll speak of fast-flowing singletracks and hurtling down steep rocky ledges—visions that send shudders down the spine of road cyclists, who want nothing better than sweet, smooth tarmac and dream of spinning for endless miles over hill and dale.

Touring cyclists crave independence and adventure, while cycling romantics want the glories of the past: climbing the famous cols from the Tour de France (page 272) or Giro d'Italia (pages 200 and 266), or tackling the legendary pavé of Paris-Roubaix (page 260). Still others want to test their mettle against the steepest hills, the highest mountain passes, or ultralong endurance events. And there are families whose idea of cycling bliss is an easy-rolling rails-to-trails path with an ice-cream stop somewhere in the middle.

To name 100 bike rides of a lifetime, I've tried to find something for everyone, be it road, gravel, or mountain bike (MTB), easy or hard, day rides or full-blown expeditions. I polled fellow cyclists and friends of friends, cycling bloggers, former pro racers, mountain bike guides, magazine editors, race organizers, cycling clubs, and custom frame builders whose clients seem to go everywhere and do everything under the sun.

Cyclists like nothing better than to gab about great rides. A few classics selected themselves, popping up with regularity: Mount Tamalpais (page 132); the Great Allegheny Passage (page 18); the gorgeous European cycling

idylls along the Loire (page 234), the Danube (page 174), and the Rhine (page 214); and, for mountain bikers, the Whole Enchilada (page 42), the crown jewel of Utah's mountain biking kingdom. A few stunners came out of left field. Mountain biking in the Yukon, anyone (page 126)? A Formula 1 track in Abu Dhabi (page 350)? Others, such as New Zealand's spectacular Lake Dunstan Trail (page 358), are brand-new, opening in 2021 to widespread acclaim.

Any book themed around a list is bound to be arbitrary and, to a degree, idiosyncratic. Readers will (hopefully) find themselves nodding in approval. But at the same time, I'm aware that there will also be scowling disapproval at my omissions. *How could he have left such and such off the list?* You have my apologies. I didn't mean to.

Ideally, though, within these pages, you will find some new rides and destinations that you hadn't heard of or considered before now. A whole world awaits on your doorstep—and there's no better way to see it than from the saddle of a bicycle.

PART ONE

THE AMERICAS

Dusk illuminates the red-rock canyonlands in the distance as a group of bikepackers traverse the Porcupine Rim portion of the Whole Enchilada in Moab, Utah (page 42).

CARRIAGE ROADS

Explore one of New England's prettiest national parks on a network of elegant roads from horse-and-buggy days.

DISTANCE: **45 miles (72 km)**   SURFACE: **Crushed gravel**   LENGTH OF TRIP: **1 to 3 days**
WHEN TO GO: **Late spring through autumn**   DIFFICULTY: **Easy**

For a man whose family wealth was founded on oil, John D. Rockefeller, Jr., showed a surprising aversion for the mechanized age. Seeking refuge from the noise and bustle of the 20th-century world he'd helped create, the billionaire heir to the Standard Oil fortune took himself off to rusticate on Maine's Mount Desert Island, where he had a secluded 100-room weekend house and thousands of acres of pristine woodland to do with as he pleased. There, in 1913, he began laying out a series of elegant horse-and-buggy carriage roads on which motorcars would be forbidden and he could tour the island's beauty spots at the leisurely pace of an already bygone age.

No expense was spared. The results were exquisite. His roads were not only beautifully engineered and wide enough for two carriages to pass unhindered, but they were also laid out with a landscaper's sympathetic eye, designed to follow the natural contours of the hills to minimize their impact. Local granite was used to build the rustic stone bridges spanning waterfalls and streams, and native vegetation such as blueberries and sweet ferns was planted along the road banks.

In all, he constructed 57 miles (92 km) of these carriage roads, some 45 miles (72 km) of which are preserved today in Acadia National Park in a

OPPOSITE: **Autumn leaves blanket a forest trail in Acadia National Park.**
PAGES 14–15: **The glacier-carved mountaintops of Cadillac Mountain in Acadia National Park**

network of loops that offers cyclists a delightful traffic-free way to explore one of America's prettiest national parks. While the roads are hardly flat, the gradients are gradual rather than steep, the crushed-gravel surfaces make for beautiful riding, and the views from the scenic lookouts are stunning. The interconnecting loops vary in distance, from Witch Hole Pond Loop at 4.7 miles (7.6 km) to the Around the Mountain Loop at 11.9 miles (19.2 km). If you're touring the carriage roads, a popular challenge is to try to ride each of the 17 individually designed stone bridges on the network. Maps of the network are available at the park visitors center, and bicycles can be rented from several places on the island if you haven't brought your own. A classic way to conclude a jaunt on the carriage roads is to stop off for tea and popovers at the Jordan Pond House restaurant, which has been something of an island mainstay since the early days of tourism in the 1890s.

BREAKOUT

The Park Loop Road—open to car traffic—makes a lovely paved 27-mile (43 km) loop of the park, with a spur going up to the summit of Cadillac Mountain. At 1,530 feet (466 m), Cadillac Mountain is the highest point along the entire eastern seaboard of the Americas, from Canada all the way down to Rio de Janeiro, and one of the first places in the United States to greet the sunrise.

BANKS-VERNONIA STATE TRAIL

A family-friendly adventure in the foothills of Oregon's coastal range and just outside the bustling city

DISTANCE: **21 miles (34 km)**   SURFACE: **Paved**   LENGTH OF TRIP: **1 day**
WHEN TO GO: **Spring through autumn (avoid August and holidays)**   DIFFICULTY: **Easy**

An approachable cycling route through the lush hills of Oregon's Coast Range, this paved trek is less than an hour's drive from Portland. The trail follows the line of the Spokane, Portland & Seattle Railway where it once ran between the town of Banks and the old timber milling town of Vernonia, some 21 miles (34 km) away, through densely wooded hills of Douglas fir, maple, and cedar.

A century ago, these woods rang to the sound of axes and the rumble of freight trains hauling timber from the state's biggest sawmill at Vernonia. The railway line, built in 1913, has long since disappeared. In its place is a seductively smooth cycle path winding through the cathedral-like forest, quiet except for the burble of mountain streams, birdsong, and the chirp of a bicycle bell. This was Oregon's first rails-to-trails project and has become one of its best loved.

It's easy to see why. In the course of pedaling its 21 miles (34 km) into the hills, you cross 13 railroad bridges, the highlight being the Buxton Trestle, towering 80 feet (24 m) above the creek below. Extend your ride with the Crown Zellerbach Trail, another rail-trail path, less than a quarter mile (0.4 km) from the Vernonia trailhead and offering another 23 miles (37 km) of superb gravel riding.

OPPOSITE: The Banks-Vernonia State Trail cuts through the trees at the Buxton Trailhead near the city of Banks in the Willamette Valley.

GREAT ALLEGHENY PASSAGE

A traffic-free run from the heart of downtown Pittsburgh through the backwoods of the Allegheny Mountains along one of America's best loved rails-to-trails paths

---

DISTANCE: 150 miles (241 km)   **SURFACE:** Mixed; mainly crushed gravel on a former railway bed
LENGTH OF TRIP: 3 to 6 days   **WHEN TO GO:** Spring through autumn   **DIFFICULTY:** Easy

The Great Allegheny Passage stretches along 150 smooth, scenic, traffic-free miles (241 km) through the Allegheny Mountains from Pittsburgh, Pennsylvania, to Cumberland, Maryland, where it joins the equally loved Chesapeake & Ohio Canal Towpath (page 54), making it possible to carry on traffic free for another 184.5 miles (297 km) all the way to Washington, D.C., with nary a hill to break your stride.

The trail starts at Point State Park in Pittsburgh, where the Monongahela and Allegheny Rivers join to form the Ohio River. Located in an area steeped in Revolutionary history, the park commemorates the unique heritage with plaques and markers throughout. The trail leads you out of town on the famous old Hot Metal Bridge, a legacy of Pittsburgh's glory days as a coke and steel town, when huge steel mills sprawled along both banks of the river. Built from 1887 through 1900, the 1,174-foot-long (358 m) railway bridge was used to ferry crucibles of molten iron from the blast furnaces on the north bank of the Monongahela to open-hearth furnaces on the south to be made into steel.

During World War II, as much as 15 percent of U.S. steel found its way across this bridge. Today the only things crossing it are pedestrians and

OPPOSITE: Bikers and runners alike cross Bollman Bridge, an 81-foot (25 m) cast- and wrought-iron truss bridge built over Wills Creek in 1871.

PAGES 20-21: A spectacular view awaits from the Salisbury Viaduct, 101 feet (30 m) above the Casselman River on the Great Allegheny Passage.

adventure-bound cyclists setting out to ride the Great Allegheny Passage.

Over the next 150 miles (241 km), the trail rolls along smoothly graded former railbeds following the Monongahela, Youghiogheny, and Casselman Rivers past a succession of old coke and steel and coal mining towns, through Pennsylvania's rustic Laurel Highlands, and over the Eastern Continental Divide, finishing just across the Mason-Dixon Line in Cumberland, Maryland.

There are no fewer than 31 railway bridges along the trail, including the towering Salisbury Viaduct, a 1,908-foot-long (582 m) trestle bridge offering stunning views down the Casselman River Valley. And where there were no easier work-arounds through the rugged Allegheny Mountains, the 19th-century railroad builders blasted tunnels—nine of them in all, the most spectacular being the 3,294-foot-long (1,004 m) Big Savage Tunnel, not far from the Continental Divide. Illuminated by ceiling

ARMCHAIR RIDE

It sounds simple: See how far you can ride a bicycle around a velodrome in an hour. And yet the Hour Record, as it is known, is said to be the toughest challenge in all of sports—one that has attracted a cavalcade of the greatest riders over the past century. Michael Hutchinson, himself an elite racer, weaves an entertaining history of the Hour and his own tilt at sporting immortality as he trains to take a crack at the record in his book *The Hour* (2006).

lights, the tunnel's cool depths can bring welcome relief from the heat on hot summer afternoons; however, because of the sharp drop in temperature, fog often forms inside, so it can be handy to have some sort of additional light.

As you near the village of Deal and the completion of the route 126 miles (203 km) after leaving Pittsburgh, you cross the Eastern Continental Divide at 2,392 feet (729 m), the highest point on the trail. Though you have to climb to get there, the trail's steepest gradient is a barely perceptible 2 percent. And from there it's pretty much a gentle downhill glide the remaining 24 miles (39 km) to Cumberland County and the finish.

DENALI NATIONAL PARK, ALASKA, U.S.A.

DENALI PARK ROAD

Experience miles of rolling arctic tundra and a plethora of wildlife on this hauntingly beautiful ride into the Alaska wilderness.

DISTANCE: **92 miles (148 km)**　　SURFACE: **Paved the first 15 miles (24 km), then gravel**
LENGTH OF TRIP: **1 to 3 days**　　WHEN TO GO: **Late spring through early autumn**　　DIFFICULTY: **Moderate**

Denali Park Road is a spectacular ribbon of highway stretching into the heart of Alaska's vast Denali National Park before dead-ending at a remote campsite within easy view—on a clear day—of the towering 20,310-foot (6,190 m) peak for which the park is named. It's a true wilderness ride, mainly on gravel, across sweeping expanses of subarctic tundra with the mountains of the Alaska Range forming a dramatic backdrop. Glimpses of moose, caribou, and grizzly bears along the way are not only possible but also likely. Best of all from a cyclist's point of view: Most of this glorious road is off-limits to private vehicles.

The road, completed in 1938, starts at the park entrance. The first 15 miles (24 km) are paved, leading you through taiga forest before breaking out into open tundra. If it's a clear day, you can catch your first glimpse of Denali, North America's highest mountain, as early as mile nine, the snowcapped peak aloof and majestic in the distance.

The pavement stops at the Savage River, as does most motorized traffic—this is generally as far as private vehicles are allowed to go. Beyond this point it's hikers and cyclists only, and the fleet of repurposed old school buses the National Park Service uses to carry visitors deeper into Denali. For the next 77 miles (124 km), it's all gravel, the road climbing up and over a succession of mountain passes as you pedal your way toward the jewel-like Wonder Lake, at mile 85, with its stunning panorama of the Alaska Range, and then to the former gold rush town of Kantishna at the end of the line.

OPPOSITE: A biker scouts the view toward Denali (formerly known as Mount McKinley) in Denali National Park.

PAGES 26-27: Cyclists enjoy the breathtaking wilderness views with the Alaska Range mountains in the background.

Several campgrounds can be found along the way. If you prefer to camp wild, you'll need to obtain a backcountry permit and attend an orientation session. You'll also have to pitch your tent at least half a mile (0.8 km) off the road and have bear-proof food canisters. On the subject of bears: Steer well clear of them. If any are lingering near the road, stop and wait for either the bear to shuffle away or a passing bus to give you and your bike a lift.

On a happier note, the park buses are fitted with bike racks, meaning you can do this stunning ride without having to backtrack, either by getting a lift out of the park or being dropped off at the end of the road and pedaling back on your own.

KNOW BEFORE YOU GO

If you want to avoid motorized traffic altogether, try going in mid-May, before the buses start operation, or mid-September, after they stop. Alternatively, you can take advantage of the midnight sun around the June solstice and ride the road through the quiet of a bright arctic night.

TOUR DE FRONDS

Wildflowers, waterfalls, and lush green forests make this challenging loop through the remote Oregon wilderness a ride to remember.

DISTANCE: **101 miles (163 km)**   SURFACE: **Paved**   LENGTH OF TRIP: **1 day**
WHEN TO GO: **Spring through autumn**   DIFFICULTY: **Challenging**

Since its first edition in 1998, the cheekily named Tour de Fronds has evolved into one of Oregon's best loved cycling events and is arguably its most beautiful as well, taking place along hauntingly quiet roads in the Coast Range. Starting and ending in the remote town of Powers, the tour's 101-mile (163 km) Cruiser Century course follows the South Fork of the Coquille River upstream, through deep old-growth forests, past banks of wildflowers, waterfalls, and rushing mountain streams, to the river's source at the head of Eden Valley, and then back again after a circuitous loop through the hills. Although the ride is fully supported, with refreshment stops at the waypoints, this is still not an easy route—there's more than 5,000 feet (1,524 m) of climbing involved—but the scenery along the way is stunning.

For those who want to enjoy all the lush greenery and cathedral forests these hills have to offer but put in a little less hard work, the Tour de Fronds offers four shorter loops of 30, 45, 63, and 77 miles (48, 72, 101, and 124 km). The event takes place on the third Saturday of each June, but for those who prefer to ride in solitude, these roads are pretty and quiet all the time. It's among the loveliest places to ride.

OPPOSITE: **This route passes through the verdant Elk Creek Falls in Rogue River–Siskiyou National Forest.**

UNDERGROUND RAILROAD ROUTE

Trace the journeys taken by thousands of freedom seekers who escaped slavery in America's antebellum South.

DISTANCE: **1,997 miles (3,214 km)**   SURFACE: **Mixed**   LENGTH OF TRIP: **1 to 2 months**
WHEN TO GO: **Summer**   DIFFICULTY: **Moderate**

Most long-distance cycling routes are simply about the challenge of pedaling a bicycle from one far-off point to another. This one tells a story, one that celebrates the daring and courage of thousands of African American freedom seekers who escaped slavery in America's antebellum South via a clandestine network of safe houses and sympathizers collectively known as the Underground Railroad. There was never any one single route on the Underground Railroad; there were many, and they were secret. This commemorative bicycle route, mapped out by the Adventure Cycling Association after much research, approximates the covert journeys taken by freedom seekers escaping plantation country in the Deep South.

The trail begins in the historic district of Mobile, Alabama, near the old slave market and Big Zion African Methodist Episcopal Zion Church, founded in 1842 and one of the city's oldest African American churches. Once clear of the city, the trail follows the same sleepy southern rivers—Alabama, Tombigbee, Tensaw, Tennessee—that guided the freedom seekers on their journeys north, taking its cue from the old African American folk song "Follow the Drinking Gourd," which advises anyone making a break for freedom to stick to the rivers—"a mighty good road"—and navigate by the stars.

OPPOSITE: A large mural depicts the history of the Underground Railroad Route's namesake.

PAGES 32-33: Paved paths make history more accessible at Tennessee's Shiloh National Military Park.

The Flight of the
GARNER FAMILY
FISCHER HOMES

For cyclists, it's pleasant pedaling through here, along the quiet, gently rolling backroads of Alabama and Mississippi—William Faulkner country—and on into the wooded hills of western Tennessee. It's the perfect scene-setter for what is to come, for once you're in Kentucky, you're in the Borderlands, the strip of land along the Ohio River marking the border between the slave states to the south and the Free States to the north. It was here that the Underground Railroad was most active and that the dangers were greatest for freedom seekers.

And it's here that you really start to encounter history, as the trail hops back and forth across the river, through historic towns such as New Albany, Madison, and Lancaster in Indiana, where museums, galleries, churches, and the restored homes of "conductors" on the Underground Railroad tell the stories of those fraught times. One of the prettiest of these waterfront towns is Ripley, Ohio, once known as Freedom's Landing, where you can visit the home of John Rankin, a Presbyterian minister who hosted an estimated 2,000 freedom seekers in his years as an Underground Railroad conductor.

CYCLING THROUGH HISTORY

One of the most daring Underground Railroad "conductors" was a former enslaved man named John P. Parker. Parker purchased his freedom in 1845 and moved to Ohio. Despite having so much to lose, he made many forays into slave country to help hundreds to safety. He was never caught and died a prosperous old man in 1900.

ABOVE: Pause for a tour of author Tennessee Williams's first home, now the Tennessee Williams House Museum and Welcome Center, in Columbus, Mississippi.

OPPOSITE: Peaceful stretches abound on the Alabama portion of the route.

From Ripley, take the 16-mile (26 km) detour to Cincinnati to see the world-class National Underground Railroad Freedom Center—a highlight of the route—and visit the Harriet Beecher Stowe House, home of the author of *Uncle Tom's Cabin*.

Ironically enough, for much of the way across Ohio, the Underground Railroad Bicycle Route follows in the tracks of an *overground* railway along the Ohio to Erie Trail, a beautiful 326-mile-long (524 km) rails-to-trails cycle path that would be a worthy inclusion on its own in a book of the world's great cycle routes. More museums, cultural centers, galleries, and historic homes and churches lie along the route as it passes through Erie, Pennsylvania, and Buffalo, New York, before coming to an end in Owen Sound, Ontario, the last stop on the Underground Railroad and where many freedom seekers settled, their long journey at an end.

GEORGE S. MICKELSON TRAIL

Explore South Dakota's legendary Black Hills along this authentic Old West railway line.

DISTANCE: **109 miles (175 km)**   SURFACE: **Gravel**   LENGTH OF TRIP: **2 to 4 days**
WHEN TO GO: **Summer through autumn**   DIFFICULTY: **Moderate**

Riding into Deadwood, South Dakota, along the George S. Mickelson Trail is like pedaling onto the set of a Western. Leaving behind the prairie town of Edgemont, the trail snakes its way into the state's legendary Black Hills along a branch line of the Chicago, Burlington & Quincy Railroad that was built back in the gold rush days of the 1880s. During the course of this 109-mile (175 km) ride, you pedal past abandoned gold mines and a ghost town, cross 100-year-old railway bridges, run through four rock tunnels, and roll for miles between cliff-lined hills clad in the dense forests that gave the Black Hills their name.

You also come within an easy detour of Custer State Park, with its grasslands and herds of buffalo, and farther along the trail, you can ride off to see two iconic stone monuments: Mount Rushmore and the Crazy Horse Memorial, a gigantic work-in-progress tribute to the Oglala warrior being carved into the granite of Thunderhead Mountain.

The first 35 miles (56 km) of the trail, heading north from Edgemont, are the quietest in terms of seeing other cyclists, as the trail rolls across the prairie toward the Black Hills. The pedaling, along a surface of smooth packed gravel, is easy. The gradients, which never exceed 4 percent along the Mickelson Trail, don't pick up until you start getting into the mountains

OPPOSITE: Bikers approach Mount Rushmore on the George S. Mickelson Trail.

PAGES 38-39: Bison graze in the sunshine at Custer State Park in South Dakota.

north of Pringle. Although the trail is never steep, some of the inclines are long.

For many, the 30-mile (48 km) section north of Hill City is the prettiest of the route, with the old railway bed following the paths of streams upward into the mountains and hugging hillsides with granite cliffs and rock spires soaring overhead. The forests are thick here, with tall stands of spruce and pine. Towering trestle bridges and keyhole-shaped tunnels blasted into the rock contribute to a sense of 19th-century railroading and Old West adventure. In early summer, meadows of wildflowers add a rush of color; in autumn, the fall foliage is spectacular.

The high point of the trail, literally—at more than 6,000 feet (1,830 m)—is just north of the Dumont trailhead. From here it is mainly downhill, a pleasant spin through forests of aspen, birch, and Black Hills spruce, 19 miles (31 km) to Deadwood and the end of the line.

CYCLING THROUGH HISTORY

Deadwood, South Dakota, is one of those brawling frontier towns that, along with Dodge City, Kansas, and Tombstone, Arizona, positively oozes Old West lore. Its most famous shooting was that of Wild Bill Hickok, gunned down by Jack McCall while playing poker in Nuttall and Mann's Saloon in 1876. Hickok was uncharacteristically sitting with his back to the door and never saw it coming. The cards he was holding at the time—two pair, black aces and black eights—have been known ever since as the "dead man's hand."

KINGS CANYON

Leave the crowds behind and explore a majestic glacial valley that 19th-century naturalist John Muir reckoned outshone Yosemite.

DISTANCE: **69 miles (111 km)**   SURFACE: **Paved**   LENGTH OF TRIP: **1 day**
WHEN TO GO: **Late spring or autumn (shoulder season and early morning)**   DIFFICULTY: **Moderate**

A stunning descent into a magnificent canyon, by some measures deeper than the Grand Canyon, is followed by exploring the valley along the wild, tumbling Kings River before pedaling back.

The ride starts at Grant Grove Village, home to the nation's second tallest sequoia, named General Grant. The first few miles are fairly sedate, an up-and-down roll through the Sierra Nevada forest that can be thought of as a buildup to the supreme moment when the canyon reveals itself. Before you know it, you're on a fast serpentine descent with sheer rocky walls towering ever higher above you.

As the road levels out near the canyon floor, you spend a few miles meandering between soaring rock formations before joining the Kings River as it splashes along its own narrow valley into a much wider, glacier-carved one, which the noted 19th-century writer and naturalist John Muir posited could eclipse Yosemite. The towering rock walls here bear a striking likeness to those of El Capitan and Half Dome.

Eventually the ride comes to a halt at the ranger station at the aptly named Road's End. Bring along a pair of walking shoes for the trail that leads to Zumwalt Meadow and the jaw-dropping views that drew 19th-century landscape painters like Albert Bierstadt. Ahead of you is the slow but equally spectacular ride back to Grant Grove Village.

OPPOSITE: **The gentle giants of Redwood Mountain Grove in Sequoia & Kings Canyon National Park**

MOAB, UTAH, U.S.A.

THE WHOLE ENCHILADA

A spicy sampler of everything Utah's world-famous mountain biking kingdom has to offer in one dramatic 8,600-foot (2,621 m) plunge to the Colorado River

DISTANCE: **27 miles (43 km)**   SURFACE: **MTB track**   LENGTH OF TRIP: **I day**
WHEN TO GO: **October**   DIFFICULTY: **Extreme**

Widely considered to be the crown jewel in Utah's mountain biking kingdom, the Whole Enchilada is a series of five seamlessly linked trails that contains everything these red-rock canyonlands have to offer distilled into one heart-stopping, adrenaline-pumping rush. People come from all over the world to do this run.

The fun starts at the Geyser Pass trailhead, in the high alpine country, about a 25-mile (40 km) shuttle ride from Moab. This is the highest of the trailheads for the Whole Enchilada, and because of the altitude and heavy snows up here, it doesn't usually open before July. At just over 10,000 feet (3,050 m), you're already plenty high enough to feel the altitude, but this is just the springboard to greater heights. From here you set off on a four-mile (6 km) climb winding your way up between the snowcapped La Sal Mountains to the crest of Burro Pass, at 11,200 feet (3,414 m). The combination of razor-thin air and gradients that approach 20 percent in places has many a rider opting for the two-legged gear on parts of this climb.

However you get to the top, pause once you're there to enjoy the magnificent views, because after this the bottom drops out as you plunge 8,600 feet (2,621 m) from alpine forests down to the bottom of the Colorado River's red sandstone canyon.

OPPOSITE: **A biker navigates challenging terrain on the Upper Porcupine Singletrack section of the Porcupine Rim Trail.**

PAGES 44–45: **Two bikers' hard work pays off with astounding views of Castle Valley outside Moab, Utah.**

At Warner Lake, near the end of the Burro Pass segment of the ride, you start a short, gnarly technical climb to the Hazard County trailhead. It's at the top of a mesa with stunning views over the red-rock canyons you'll be descending, as well as offering a backward glance at the La Sal Mountains through which you just passed.

The descent from here is fast and flowing, with the Hazard County Trail widening and becoming the doubletrack Kokopelli Trail, which in turn leads onto the Upper and then the Lower Porcupine Singletrack. This hugs the rim of Porcupine Canyon and offers a bit of everything in terms of riding challenges: plunges, swooping turns, and classic Moab slickrock. And more great views too, if you have the nerve to look away for an instant to see them.

Lower Porcupine Singletrack is where you encounter the crux move on the Whole Enchilada: the Notch, a harrowing descent down a stony gully that would give a mountain goat

ALTERNATE ROUTE

The Magnificent Seven offers an exhilarating 26-mile (42 km) sweep of singletrack through Moab's stunning red-rock landscapes. As the name implies, the Magnificent Seven is a cobbling together of seven trails: Bull Run, Arth's Corner, Little Canyon, Gold Bar Rim, Golden Spike, Poison Spider, and Portal, each of which is an epic ride in its own right. Portal, a double-black-diamond trail, is especially technical and intimidating; take great care, or end your ride with Poison Spider as many do.

pause. This section in particular is for experts only, requiring a high commitment and having potentially high consequences if you miss your line. With this in mind, the majority of riders choose to walk their bikes down this section or take the (slightly) easier alternative known as the Snotch.

After this comes the fast, flowy 11-mile (18 km) ride along Porcupine Rim to the Colorado River. The views are stunning, but this is still a highly technical descent. There's no letup anywhere and you need to be on your game the whole way.

From the finish, you can either ride the five miles (8 km) back to town on a combination of public road and bicycle path or arrange for a shuttle transfer. October is the best time to do the Whole Enchilada—after summer has lost its heat but before the snow starts. Whatever time of year, be prepared for sudden changes in weather.

KETTLE VALLEY RAIL TRAIL

Ride through some of the wildest and most rugged sections of the Canadian Rockies along Canada's most spectacular rails-to-trails path.

DISTANCE: **134 miles (216 km)**   SURFACE: **Gravel**   LENGTH OF TRIP: **2 to 3 days**
WHEN TO GO: **June through October**   DIFFICULTY: **Easy to moderate**

When civil engineers for the Canadian Pacific Railway laid out the tracks for its first transcontinental line in the early 1880s, they opted for a more northerly route through British Columbia to save themselves the expense of putting a line through the dense pocket of mountains that lie to the south. A big silver strike a few years later changed all that. With thousands of American prospectors pouring into these mountains, getting their supplies and shipping out their silver ore through the much more convenient railhead at Spokane, provincial authorities decided to act—if for no other reason than to preserve Canadian sovereignty over the region.

It took more than 20 years to get off the ground and build, and was among the costliest stretch of railway per mile in North America, but by 1915 the Kettle Valley Railway was up and running, snaking through the mountains and alongside precipitous gorges, servicing the isolated mining towns and timber mills and fruit-growing region around Okanagan Lake. Jump forward a century, and bicycles have long since replaced trains on what is now one of Canada's most spectacular rails-to-trails routes, winding some 300 miles (483 km) through the mountains from Midway to Hope.

The 134-mile (216 km) stretch from Midway to Penticton offers some of the

OPPOSITE: **A lengthy trestle bridge in Myra Canyon near Kelowna, British Columbia, Canada**

PAGES 50-51: **Vineyards and beautiful water views dot the landscape near Penticton on the Kettle Valley Rail Trail.**

finest scenery the route has to offer—in particular the dramatic Myra Canyon segment, with its 18 trestle bridges, some of them towering hundreds of feet above the canyon floor, and two mountain tunnels.

It's a gravel track more suitable for mountain and gravel bikes than tourers. From the starting point in Midway, you roll through 10 miles (16 km) or so of farmland along the Kettle River before the long but gentle climb into the mountains. The gradient is no more than 2.2 percent—trains don't like steep grades any more than touring cyclists do. As you ascend higher and deeper into the mountains, the trail takes on a wilder aspect. Encounters with bears, wolves, mountain lions, and rattlesnakes are not unheard of up here. Seventy-five miles (121 km) into your journey, you reach Myra Canyon and its spectacular series of trestle bridges and tunnels. After Chute Lake, you begin a jaunty descent into Penticton, its cultivated landscapes of vineyards and orchards a mellow counterpoint to the rugged wilderness through which you've just passed, making for a splendid end to your adventure.

ALTERNATE ROUTE

Looking for something bigger? The Kettle Valley Rail Trail is part of the Great Trail (aka Trans Canada Trail), a vast network of more than 15,000 miles (24,140 km) of backroads, cycle paths, and waterways stretching from the Atlantic to the Pacific and north to the Arctic Ocean. It is the longest multiuse trail network in the world and takes in every part of Canada.

EMPIRE STATE TRAIL

Shuffle off to Buffalo on this nearly traffic-free trail that stretches from the heart of Manhattan across New York State.

DISTANCE: **560 miles (901 km) NYC to Buffalo; 399 miles (642 km) NYC to Canadian border**
SURFACE: **Mixed; paved, crushed gravel**   LENGTH OF TRIP: **10 to 14 days to Buffalo; 7 to 10 days to Canadian border**   WHEN TO GO: **May through October**   DIFFICULTY: **Easy to moderate**

W hat a way to escape the city! Imagine being able to set off right from Manhattan on a long-haul cycling adventure across the entire state of New York, happy in the knowledge that the vast majority of your journey is going to unfold on safe, traffic-free cycle paths. It seems a dream, but thanks to the new Empire State Trail (opened in 2021), you can now do exactly that. Starting from the Battery, within sight of the Statue of Liberty, you can shuffle off to Buffalo, and 85 percent of your pedaling en route can be done on easy-to-ride cycle paths.

Or alternately, when you reach Albany, you can bear to the right, take the northern extension of the Empire State Trail, and ride up to Lake Champlain on the Canadian border for a considerably hillier journey that will be roughly 55 percent traffic free overall.

Resembling a sideways T on a map of New York State, the Empire State Trail comprises three very different segments: the Hudson River Valley Greenway Trail, which takes you from downtown New York City to Albany; the Erie Canalway Trail, which runs from Albany to Buffalo; and the Champlain Valley Trail, which stretches from Albany some 199 miles (320 km) north through the Adirondacks and on to Rouses Point on the Canadian border. Together they total 750 miles (1,207 km). For those who like to wrap their touring around a theme, more than 200 craft breweries can be found along the length of the trail. There is even a mobile app to help you find them.

BREAKOUT

As a warm-up to your New York State adventure, or simply as a grand adventure on its own, do a tour of Manhattan on the Manhattan Waterfront Greenway, a 31-mile (50 km) cycle path looping around the island from Battery Park in the south, along the Hudson River, up to Harlem, and then back again along the East River.

OPPOSITE: Fall is a picturesque season for cycling in Pittsford, New York, on the Empire State Trail.

CHESAPEAKE & OHIO CANAL TOWPATH

A rustic ride from the nation's capital deep into the Appalachian Mountains along the towpath of a historic canal—traffic free all the way

DISTANCE: 185 miles (298 km)   **SURFACE:** Unpaved   **LENGTH OF TRIP:** 3 to 5 days
WHEN TO GO: Autumn   **DIFFICULTY:** Easy

Like the Great Allegheny Passage (page 18), with which it is often paired, the Chesapeake & Ohio Canal Towpath is a much loved long-distance cycling path, stretching 184.5 blissfully traffic-free miles (297 km) from the heart of Washington, D.C., to Cumberland, Maryland.

There it connects seamlessly with the Great Allegheny Passage, making it possible to pedal all the way from the Potomac River to Pittsburgh—a total distance of 333 miles (536 km)—on woodsy cycle paths with no traffic and nary a hill to break your stride. You simply hop on your bike in Georgetown and follow the Potomac upstream and into the hinterlands along the old canal path, through a long corridor of parkland with stops along the way at historic towns such as Harpers Ferry, West Virginia, at mile 62.

Because these two trails flow into each other so smoothly and are often ridden back-to-back by long-haul tourers, it's tempting in a book like this to combine them in a single entry. But that wouldn't be fair to either of these lovely paths. They are very different, with different histories and different characteristics, and offer different cycling experiences.

For starters the C&O isn't a rails-to-trails route but an old towpath dating from the 1820s, trodden by mules pulling heavily laden freight barges down from the Allegheny Mountains along the banks of a canal. The path itself is

OPPOSITE: Speeding along the Chesapeake & Ohio Canal Towpath

PAGES 56-57: The Chesapeake & Ohio Canal Towpath crosses under a bridge in Georgetown in Washington, D.C.

rougher, woodsier, lonelier, with more roots and rocks to negotiate than you'd find spinning along from town to town on a smooth crushed-gravel railbed. Though you could get away with riding the Great Allegheny Passage on a lightweight tourer, a knobby-tired gravel bike is the much better option on the C&O. But this rusticity adds to the path's charm, as do its old locks, dams, aqueducts, and lockkeepers' cottages that you pass along the way.

The Grand Old Ditch, as the canal was known, operated between 1850 and 1924 and was regarded as an engineering marvel in its day. To float a barge from sea level in Washington to Cumberland's 610-foot (186 m) elevation in the Allegheny Mountains, engineers had to design and build 74 locks and 11 aqueducts. The really big-ticket item was the construction of the 3,118-foot-long (950 m) Paw Paw Tunnel, which saved six miles (9.6 km) of canal building by allowing boats to float *through* a mountain ridge rather than around it. Lined with six million bricks and taking 14 years to build, the tunnel cost so much that it nearly drove the project into bankruptcy. Today pedaling through the old canal tunnel—at mile 155—is one of the highlights of the ride.

THE BAJA DIVIDE

Find endless miles of Old West adventure in the remote desert
wilds south of the border.

DISTANCE: 1,673 miles (2,692 km)   **SURFACE:** Mixed; paved, gravel, rock, soft sand
LENGTH OF TRIP: 6 to 8 weeks   **WHEN TO GO:** November through March   **DIFFICULTY:** Challenging to extreme

A hidden gem waiting just south of the border, Baja offers seemingly endless miles of remote desert tracks, desolate coastlines, sparkling seas, mountain ranges, wild camping, and a sense of escaping into the pages of an Old West adventure. While it is possible to follow the paved Highway 1 all the way down to the tip of the peninsula, the real adventure starts on the rugged backcountry tracks that connect remote fishing villages and ranches. These tracks are often unnamed and lacking signage, so you'll need a good set of maps, either in your panniers or downloaded to your GPS.

You'll need a sturdy bicycle as well—something more than just a standard mountain bike: one with fat three-inch tires (at least) to cope with stretches of deep sand. This is seriously remote riding. In the backcountry here, expect to carry a three-day supply of food between towns and at least two to three gallons (7.5 to 11 L) of water. Most small towns and marketplaces in Baja have purified-water refill stations where you can fill up your bottles with clean water at nominal charge. The deserts here are searingly hot in summer, so go in the winter months. If you're lucky, you may spot some whales in these secluded waters.

OPPOSITE: A fully packed
touring bike is ready for a
day on the Baja Divide trail.

NEW RIVER TRAIL

Follow an old railway line through the musical heart of bluegrass country in rural Appalachia.

DISTANCE: **57 miles (92 km)** SURFACE: **Crushed rock; former railway bed**
LENGTH OF TRIP: **1 to 3 days** WHEN TO GO: **August** DIFFICULTY: **Easy**

This one is for lovers of old-timey bluegrass music. One of the world's oldest rivers, the New River guides you through the musical heart of rural Appalachia along what used to be a branch line of the old Norfolk & Western Railway.

Galax, Virginia, the starting point for the ride, is said to have produced more fiddlers and banjo pickers than any other town in America. Indeed, one such local band, the Hill Billies, popular on the radio back in the 1920s, lent its name to "hillbilly" music. Today the town is home to the Blue Ridge Music Center (open May to October), a museum that is dedicated to mountain music and that offers interactive exhibitions, live performances, and storytelling in the afternoons, and a series of Saturday evening concerts throughout the summer.

The bicycle path starts beside the red caboose on the edge of town and runs for the first 12 miles (19 km) through a narrow, heavily wooded valley before joining the New River, crossing it on a 1,089-foot-long (332 m) wooden trestle bridge. Once on the other side, you have the option of taking an 11-mile (18 km) round-trip side trip—this distance is included in the overall length of the ride—that follows the river upstream on the old spur line to Fries. It's a pleasant diversion, and for bluegrass lovers it offers another chance to touch base with history.

It was from Fries, back in 1923, that an aspiring young musician named Henry Whitter set off for New York City, banjo in hand, having quit his job at a textile mill in the hope of making it big as a recording artist. And this he

OPPOSITE: Pausing to take in the view along the New River Trail

PAGES 62–63: The Blue Ridge Mountains in Galax, Virginia

did, becoming one of America's first bluegrass and country music stars. Among the tracks he cut on his first album was a song titled, appropriately enough, "The New River Train."

For modern cyclists Fries is a good place to top off your water bottles and grab a bite to eat. The next 39 miles (63 km) to Pulaski are fairly remote, as the path wends its way along the densely wooded valley. The pedaling is easy, on a nearly level gravel path, and the New River makes for a pleasant riding companion, one whose moods vary from sleepy and restful to cheerful rapids.

As you head downstream, you cross dozens of trestle bridges, ride through two tunnels, and pass a shot tower dating from 1807 that made musket balls and buckshot back in the day. As you approach the town of Pulaski, you cross the 951-foot (290 m) Hiwassee River Bridge.

The New River Trail is brightened by wildflowers in spring, and in autumn the fall foliage is glorious. But for bluegrass lovers, the best time to come is in August for the Old Fiddlers' Convention in Galax, an annual fixture since 1935 that draws competitors and spectators from all over the country.

REST STOP

Those looking for adventure can find it in New River Gorge National Park in West Virginia. Here the sleepy New River becomes a roaring cataract through a spectacular gorge, spanned by the New River Gorge Bridge. Each year on Bridge Day (in October), the bridge is closed to traffic while thrill-seeking adventurers rappel and BASE jump from its dizzying heights.

WASATCH CREST TRAIL

Stunning mountain views and adrenaline-burning descents in Utah's high country

DISTANCE: 18 miles (29 km)   **SURFACE:** Gravel, rock   **LENGTH OF TRIP:** 1 day
WHEN TO GO: June for the wildflowers; September for the foliage   **DIFFICULTY:** Challenging

Explore the high country in one of Utah's most beautiful mountain ranges with this iconic run of high-altitude singletracks offering jaw-dropping views, plunging descents, and tricky technical sections. The classic route starts at Guardsman Pass near the Solitude ski resort. A breezy run of singletrack snakes through the aspens on banked curves before it drops down through a stand of pines. The views are breathtaking—literally, since Guardsman Pass is at 9,717 feet (2,961 m).

A mile and a half (2.4 km) of riding brings you to the day's first challenge: the ascent of aptly named Puke Hill. This brutal little rise may not be long, but it sure is steep, gaining 350 feet (107 m) in less than half a mile (0.8 km). But there's a payoff. On the other side is some of the most spectacular mountain biking in the West. Once over the crest, you spin along a ridgeline with gorgeous long views as you slalom through the aspens. In June you can add kaleidoscopic banks of wildflowers to the mix as well.

This exhilarating run delivers you to the narrow and exposed ridge known as the Spine. Here you may wish to dismount and walk the bike.

Not far past the Spine, the trail forks. Bear to the left to Desolation Lake and the Mill D North Fork, a singletrack ride into Cottonwood Canyon. Bear to the right to finish via Millcreek Canyon—be advised that bicycles are allowed into this canyon only on even-numbered days.

KNOW BEFORE YOU GO

Bear in mind that this trail is at altitude, and the weather can change abruptly. Prepare for anything.

OPPOSITE: Three riders pause atop a rocky crest outside Park City, Utah.

TRANSAMERICA TRAIL

A classic—perhaps *the* classic—all-American coast-to-coast bicycle route

DISTANCE: **4,218 miles (6,788 km)**   SURFACE: **Mixed**   LENGTH OF TRIP: **2 to 3 months**
WHEN TO GO: **Summer through autumn**   DIFFICULTY: **Challenging**

D reamed up in a whirl of idealism in the 1970s, when the United States was enjoying a cycling boom and looking ahead to its bicentennial, the TransAmerica Trail is a glorious way to discover the country intimately, from small town to small town, from the redwood forest to the Blue Ridge Mountains.

As a point-to-point ride, the TransAmerica Trail can be ridden in either direction, although most thru-riders start in the West, the idea being to take advantage of prevailing winds. Although the truth of the matter is that winds are fickle; depending on your luck, you can have headwinds or tailwinds whichever way you go. A better and more surprising reason to ride from west to east is to get a few thousand miles in your legs before you tackle the *really* hilly portions of the trail, which aren't, as you might imagine, in the Rocky Mountains but in the gnarly old Appalachians toward the end of your ride. There's more granny-gearing on the backroads of Virginia than there is on any other portion of the trail.

And so for most, the journey begins in Astoria, a picturesque town near the mouth of the Columbia River in Northwest Oregon. From there the trail heads south 100 miles (161 km) along the spectacular coastal highway before veering inland toward bicycle-friendly Eugene (pop. 175,000), the biggest town you will encounter on the entire crossing, and on through

OPPOSITE: **The orange-painted landscape spreads wide as a biker descends into a valley on the Ely Highway outside Milford, Utah.**

PAGES 68-69: **A rider's bike and tent balance above the Rocky Mountains at the summit of Monarch Pass.**

the snowcapped Cascades via the mile-high (1.6 km) McKenzie Pass.

After crossing Oregon's arid eastern plains, the trail takes a circuitous course through the rugged wilderness of the Idaho Panhandle and over Lolo Pass to Montana before tracking south and into two of America's most spectacular national parks—Yellowstone and Grand Teton. Then it passes through Wyoming's hauntingly desolate basin country, the biggest of Big Sky country.

From there, it's on to Colorado and the Rockies, pedaling up and over the 11,542-foot (3,518 m) Hoosier Pass, which marks the literal high point of the journey. Pueblo, Colorado, the second largest town along the trail, is a good place to stock up before the long stretches of empty road ahead as you cross

CYCLING THROUGH HISTORY

As you pedal your way across the Great Plains, tip your hat to the 25th Infantry Regiment Bicycle Corps, an African American unit known as the Buffalo Soldiers, who in 1897 pedaled more than 1,900 miles (3,060 km) from Fort Missoula, Montana, to St. Louis, Missouri. On heavy single-speed bicycles with full Army kit and rifles, they braved torrential rain, mud, snow, and freezing temperatures yet covered more than 50 miles (80 km) a day, arriving in St. Louis 41 days later, where they were greeted by 1,000 local cyclists who escorted them into the city.

ABOVE: The TransAmerica Trail passes by the B. F. Major storefront in Sebree, Kentucky.

OPPOSITE: A young boy and his cow at the 2020 Greenwood County Fair animal auction in Eureka, Kansas—a worthwhile stop.

the eastern Colorado Piedmont and the endlessly open, flat Kansas farmlands.

Missouri brings with it roller-coaster hills through the Ozark Mountains and plenty of Civil War sites. You cross the Mississippi River at Chester, Illinois, and not long afterward take a ferry across the Ohio River and enter the blue-grass country of Kentucky, with its horse farms and white fences. Then the trail heads into the Appalachians, with those steep, gnarly hills and twisting backroads. A spin along a stretch of Virginia's stunning Blue Ridge Parkway (page 94) leads down into fertile farmlands and plantations and landscapes rich in colonial history, finishing up in Yorktown, on the Chesapeake Bay, the end of your journey. Dip your wheel in the Atlantic and congratulate yourself on completing an epic ride.

LA FAROLA

A dramatic ride over the mountains to Cuba's oldest tropical seaside town

DISTANCE: **37 miles (59 km)**   SURFACE: **Paved**   LENGTH OF TRIP: **1 day**
WHEN TO GO: **November through April**   DIFFICULTY: **Challenging**

Said to be the most beautiful road in Cuba, La Farola takes you on a stunning roller coaster of a ride from the southern part of the island, over a spine of mountains, through a hauntingly beautiful cloud forest, and then to the historic seaport of Baracoa, once the most isolated town in Cuba.

It starts at the small beach town of Cajobabo, about 125 miles (200 km) east of Santiago de Cuba, and zigzags up the side of the mountains on La Farola road. The road was built in the early 1960s, not long after the Cuban Revolution, and was regarded as an engineering marvel in its day, crossing the formidable Sierra del Purial mountains.

Straightaway, you'll notice the change in scenery and ecosystems as you climb upward. The cacti and aloe growing along the arid Caribbean coast give way to mango trees, royal palms, and lush ferns. By the time this serpentine road crests the pass, at Alto de Cotilla, after a climb of nearly 2,000 feet (610 m), you're pedaling through scented forests of Cuban pines. If you feel your energy levels flagging, there's no shortage of fruit stands selling mangoes, bananas, and *cucuruchos*—a classic sweet made with grated coconut, honey, and a blend of local tropical fruits, all wrapped in a palm leaf.

And then the descent begins, fast and breezy down the northern flank of the mountains, through tropical rainforests and El Jamal Valley, famous for its cacao plantations, all the way down to Baracoa, the original capital of Cuba, founded by the Spanish conquistador Diego Velázquez de Cuéllar in 1511. It's a worthy end point for the journey.

OPPOSITE: La Farola's path cuts between Cajobabo and Baracoa, Cuba.

OLD MISSION PENINSULA TRAIL

Cherry orchards, vineyards, sparkling beaches, and a historic lighthouse add up to an unforgettable ride along the shores of Lake Michigan.

DISTANCE: **36 miles (58 km)**   SURFACE: **Paved**   LENGTH OF TRIP: **1 day**
WHEN TO GO: **Summer through autumn**   DIFFICULTY: **Easy**

This one's perfect for gourmands! Starting in Traverse City, Michigan, the tart-cherry capital of the United States, the route makes a looping 36-mile (58 km) round trip to the historic lighthouse at the tip of the Old Mission Peninsula, in Grand Traverse Bay on Lake Michigan, and back. It passes through a gently rolling countryside of cherry orchards and vineyards—the area is also known for its wines. The narrowness of the peninsula (barely four miles/two kilometers at its widest) coupled with the weather-moderating effects of the lake have created a microclimate that's ideal for varietals such as Chardonnay, Riesling, and Pinot Noir. The 10 wineries on the peninsula offer tastings and light bites, and farm shops between the wineries sell cherries and all manner of related products. The route generally hugs the coast, offering lovely lake views that repay the effort needed to climb the few steep hills along the way. The turnaround point is the Mission Point Lighthouse, built in 1870 and straddling the 45th parallel of north latitude, exactly halfway between the Equator and the North Pole. Old Mission Peninsula Lighthouse Park offers several miles of developed trails and is next to one of the area's prettiest beaches, Haserot Beach. Traverse City has long been famous for hosting the National Cherry Festival in July, an annual event since 1925 that draws half a million visitors.

OPPOSITE: **The multiuse TART (Traverse Area Recreation and Transportation) Trails in Traverse City, Michigan**

RAGBRAI

An Iowa tradition dating back half a century, this annual midsummer ride across the state celebrates the best of small-town America.

DISTANCE: **468 miles (753 km)** SURFACE: **Paved** LENGTH OF TRIP: **7 days**
WHEN TO GO: **July** DIFFICULTY: **Moderate**

n 1973 two newspaper journalists from the *Des Moines Register* decided to cycle across Iowa, from Sioux City to Davenport, writing stories along the way. They published their route in advance and invited their readers to join them. Much to their surprise, some 300 did—including an 83-year-old man who wore a pith helmet and pedaled a much used ladies' Schwinn bicycle.

Hundreds more readers wrote in saying they would have liked to come along but hadn't been able to get away on short notice. And so the newspaper promised to do another ride the following summer. This they did, to even greater acclaim, with 2,700 riders showing up at the start. When a third running of the event proved more popular still, a tradition was born: the Register's Annual Great Bicycle Ride Across Iowa—or RAGBRAI, as it's known.

Half a century later RAGBRAI has grown into a beloved fixture on the annual cycle-touring calendar, drawing thousands of riders from all 50 states and overseas. The route varies from year to year, but always traverses the entire state, west to east, from the Missouri River to the Mississippi. The average distance covered is about 470 miles (755 km), with the event spread across seven days.

Eight host towns are selected for the overnight stops along the way. Camping space is provided, along with live music and plenty of opportunities to buy food and drinks. A carnival atmosphere prevails. During the day, the

OPPOSITE: Cornfields and farmlands span the 2017 RAGBRAI route.

PAGES 78-79: A verdant stretch of the 2015 RAGBRAI

dreamy backroads of Iowa are sparkling with thousands of cyclists. Entire towns turn out to greet them, with more live music on the streets, and the best of local cooking and produce on offer. The Iowa Corn Growers Association even hands out free hot, buttered corn on the cob to passing cyclists. This is a celebration of everything good about Iowa and small-town America.

From its informal beginnings in the 1970s, RAGBRAI has evolved into a smartly run operation—one that includes roving mechanics to fix troublesome bikes, first-aid stations, and a sag wagon to give weary stragglers a lift at the end of the day to that night's destination.

The event is so popular that entries must now be limited to 8,500. Day passes are also available if you can't spare an

CYCLING THROUGH HISTORY

After RAGBRAI co-founder John Karras died in 2021 at age 91, organizers decided to honor his memory and love of long-distance rides by incorporating a 100-mile (161 km) day, called Century Day, into the event. It adds to the challenge and spirit of adventure (though those who can't complete the Century ride can get a lift to the finish). It's a fitting tribute to a man who first conceived the idea of RAGBRAI during the course of a 125-mile (201 km) ride from Des Moines to Iowa City in 1971.

ABOVE: The Moy family—
Prow Sarnsethsiri and her
children, Veronica (7),
Justin (13), and Nicholas
(12)—prepare to enjoy the
annual RAGBRAI race.

OPPOSITE: An overhead
view of cyclists in Lidder-
dale, Iowa, in the annual
RAGBRAI

entire week for the ride. Passes are available for support crew as well, so they can have access to camping and those end-of-day festivities no one wants to miss.

At the same time, for all its festive atmosphere, RAGBRAI is still a serious ride, covering 468 miles (753 km) of wide-open Iowa landscape from the bluffs of the Missouri River to the banks of the Mississippi—it's a proper adventure. Summer temperatures can top 100°F (37°C), and there can just as easily be winds and rain, so be sure to bring appropriate gear and pack plenty of water. Among the many other things you will learn about Iowa over the course of this weeklong ride: The state ain't flat!

CRATER LAKE SCENIC RIM DRIVE

Ride around one of the most beautiful lakes in the country.

DISTANCE: 33 miles (53 km)   **SURFACE: Paved**   **LENGTH OF TRIP: 1 day**
WHEN TO GO: September   **DIFFICULTY: Challenging**

Nestled in the caldera of a sleeping volcano high in Oregon's Cascade Mountains, jewel-like Crater Lake ranks among the world's deepest lakes, at 1,949 feet (594 m), and its sapphire waters are considered among the world's purest. It is the centerpiece of one of America's oldest and most popular national parks. Riding a loop of the scenic mountain road that encircles the lake is high on many a cyclist's bucket list.

The route follows the park's Rim Drive, a hilly, breathtakingly beautiful drive that, as its name implies, runs along the rim of the caldera, several hundred feet above the lake. The entire ride is at altitude—it varies from 6,500 to 7,877 feet (1,980 to 2,401 m)—which, together with the road's steep grades, makes this a challenging ride. But the views more than repay the effort, and with 30 scenic lookouts along the way, there are plenty of opportunities to stop and admire—and catch your breath.

The lake and the towering walls of the caldera that surround it are the result of a catastrophic eruption of Mount Mazama some 7,700 years ago. The eruption blasted 12 cubic miles (50 cubic km) of rock into the sky, sending

OPPOSITE: **A cyclist circles Crater Lake on the Crater Lake Scenic Rim Drive.**

PAGES 84-85: **Dawn along the caldera rim of Oregon's Crater Lake National Park**

ash across eight states and three Canadian provinces, and reduced the height of the original mountain from an estimated 12,000 feet (3,660 m) to 8,157 feet (2,486 m) today. Over the following 700 years as the forests regenerated, runoff rainwater and snowmelt created the astonishingly beautiful lake in the volcano's crater.

Crater Lake receives some serious amounts of snowfall during the winter—the annual average is just under 500 inches (1,270 cm)—so the Rim Drive is open for only a few months a year, typically July to October. Given the park's popularity, prepare for the road to be busy with sightseers—go early in the morning if you can. Or better still, if your holiday plans allow it, do this gem of a ride during the two special cycling weekends the park offers each September, when the 24-mile (39 km) East Rim section of the route is closed to motor traffic and becomes a delightful high-altitude cycling idyll.

ALTERNATE ROUTE

If you fancy a dip in those startling blue waters, or just want to stand along the shore, you can do it, although there's only one access point: the Cleetwood Cove Trail, which starts from a prominent viewpoint 4.6 miles (7.4 km) east of the north entrance to the park. It's a steep and strenuous hike down a narrow switchback trail that drops 700 feet (213 m) in just a little over a mile. Bring plenty of water and sunscreen, and wear sturdy shoes. The water is chilly too, even in summer, so pack something warm to change into.

TRAIL OF THE COEUR D'ALENES

Cross the wild and beautiful panhandle of northern Idaho along the line of an old railway built for the 19th-century silver mines.

DISTANCE: **73 miles (117 km)**   SURFACE: **Paved cycle track**   LENGTH OF TRIP: **1 to 2 days**
WHEN TO GO: **Summer**   DIFFICULTY: **Easy**

One of the most scenic rails-to-trails routes in the American West, the Trail of the Coeur d'Alenes spans the Idaho Panhandle along an old Union Pacific railbed that dates back to the silver mining days of the 1880s. Starting near the Washington-Idaho border in Plummer, you spin along the western end of the trail through the foothills of the Palouse Prairie and then over the southern end of Lake Coeur d'Alene on the spectacular 3,100-foot-long (945 m) Chatcolet trestle swing-span bridge, built by the railroad in 1921.

The lakeside resort town of Harrison is a good place to grab lunch or an ice cream and refill your water bottles, as there is no potable water farther along the trail. From Harrison, you follow the Coeur d'Alene River along a scenic chain of lakes, rich in wildlife and waterfowl, and then head through Silver Valley, where veins of silver, lead, and zinc sparked a mining boom in 1884. Old mining towns near the trail, such as Wallace, Kellogg, and Cataldo, offer places to stay and break your journey.

OPPOSITE: **A rainbow touches down on a vividly red barn at a farm in the Palouse hills of northern Idaho.**

THE GREAT DIVIDE

Take on a rugged mountain bike challenge from the high country in the
Canadian Rockies to the desert along the Mexican border.

DISTANCE: **3,088 miles (4,970 km)**   SURFACE: **Mixed; mostly gravel, off-road**
LENGTH OF TRIP: **2 months**   WHEN TO GO: **July**   DIFFICULTY: **Extreme**

One of the world's longest mountain biking routes, the Great Divide Mountain Bike Route (GDMBR) runs along the spine of the Continental Divide from the high alpine meadows of the Canadian Rockies to the rattlesnake desert on the Mexican border. Along its 3,088-mile (4,970 km) length, you pass through some of North America's most spectacular wilderness areas and two of its best loved national parks: Yellowstone and Yosemite.

With much of the trail remote and unpaved, taking riders to altitudes of nearly 12,000 feet (3,660 m) and involving a total of more than 200,000 feet (60,960 m) of elevation gain, this is not one for the faint of heart. Snow is a possibility on the high mountain passes. So are fearsome mountain thunderstorms, with machine-gun hail, torrential rains, and lightning. Mosquitoes are a fact of life. Oh, you'll definitely need to carry bear spray as well and keep it within easy reach—encounters with grizzlies are not at all unknown. But as a bike ride of a lifetime, it doesn't get much bigger, grander, or more challenging than the GDMBR.

Managed by the Adventure Cycling Association, the trail crosses the Continental Divide no fewer than 26 times and passes through a cavalcade

OPPOSITE: Terrie Clouse,
former U.S.A. Cycling
Masters road national
champion, leaves
Wyoming's Union
Pass behind on the
Great Divide Mountain
Bike Route.

PAGES 90-91: Wildflowers
line Road 401 south of
Rawlins on the Great Divide
Mountain Bike Route.

of glorious western landscapes—alpine meadows, deep forests, secluded river valleys, open grasslands, high plains, and a magnificent expanse of the Chihuahuan Desert.

Highlights include Canada's remote Flathead River Valley (serious bear country!); Wyoming's desolate Wind River Range, one of the loveliest alpine stretches of the route; and New Mexico's Gila Wilderness, with the literal high point of the ride being the 11,910-foot (3,630 m) Indiana Pass in the Colorado Rockies.

For southbound riders—and most thru-riders travel north to south—the journey starts in Jasper, in the Canadian Rockies. As you head south into Montana, the climbs become longer, the forests taller, and the trails wilder. Occasionally the route dips down from the high country into small towns where you can replenish supplies.

The trail enters Wyoming near Yellowstone and Grand Teton National Parks; leads you

ALTERNATE ROUTE

If you're short on time and long on ambition—to say nothing of being extraordinarily fit, self-reliant, and capable on a bike—you can always try tackling the Tour Divide: riding the entire length of the Great Divide Mountain Bike Route as a time-trial race. It's an annual event. The Grand Depart, from Banff, takes place the second Friday in June. The clock starts the moment you set off and doesn't stop until you roll up to the finish line on the Mexican border. Top riders will average 175 miles (282 km) a day. There's no entry fee, no formal registration, and no prizes either. It's all for the glory.

ABOVE: Trail markers for the Colorado Trail and Continental Divide Trail

OPPOSITE: The Great Divide Mountain Bike Route between San Mateo Spring and Ojo Frio spring, New Mexico

through the beautifully desolate Wind River Range; goes along the divide itself and down through the Old West ghost town of South Pass City; and then heads on to the Great Divide Basin. Water is scarce here, so carry plenty—three gallons (11 L) is not an unreasonable amount.

Colorado is where the serious climbs are, with long ascents starting at 8,000 feet (2,438 m), passing through beautiful alpine meadows and stands of aspens and into western towns and glitzy ski resorts.

As you head into New Mexico, the pedaling surfaces become rougher, and the climate more arid, although subject to afternoon thunderstorms, which can turn a dusty track into a quagmire of unrideable mud. This is one of the most remote sections of the journey, and among the most beautiful, as you cross the wilds of the Chihuahuan Desert to the finish line in Antelope Wells.

BLUE RIDGE PARKWAY

Spin along America's favorite highway for hundreds of miles through the woods without a single stop sign.

DISTANCE: **469 miles (755 km)**   SURFACE: **Paved**   LENGTH OF TRIP: **10 to 14 days**
WHEN TO GO: **Summer through autumn**   DIFFICULTY: **Challenging**

Affectionately called "America's Favorite Drive," the Blue Ridge Parkway, built in 1936, runs along the crest of the southern Appalachian Mountains, linking two beautiful national parks: Shenandoah in Virginia and Great Smoky Mountains in North Carolina. The road itself is the nation's longest linear park and the most visited of any of the U.S. National Park Service's offerings, with more than 15 million people traveling the parkway each year. Many thousands of these are cyclists.

It's a stunning ride, an unbroken ribbon of bitumen flowing through some of rural Appalachia's most striking backcountry and the highest mountains east of the Mississippi. From the moment you join the parkway, near Afton, Virginia, until you finally leave it some 469 miles (755 km) later in Cherokee, North Carolina, you won't see a single stoplight, roundabout, or stop sign. No trucks either, and the speed limit for cars is a sedate 45 miles an hour (72 km/h). At the same time, the Blue Ridge is no cakewalk. Riding the length of the parkway involves nearly 49,000 feet (14,935 m) of elevation gain, and while there are plenty of camping opportunities along the route, its long, lonely stretches mean you need to give thought in advance to where you can obtain food and water. It is possible to leave the parkway

OPPOSITE: A camera mounted to a mountain bike atop a car captures a section of the Blue Ridge Parkway north of Asheville, North Carolina.

PAGES 96-97: Ravens Roost Overlook on the Blue Ridge Parkway

and drop down into towns along the way, but this can sometimes add quite a bit of distance, and occasionally the climbs back up onto the Blue Ridge can be astonishingly steep.

The Virginia portion takes you through rolling farmland and forests and along picturesque river valleys with long, serpentine climbs over the hills. Indeed, the longest climb on the journey is here, a 13-mile-long (21 km) slog from the banks of the James River to the top of Apple Orchard Mountain, which, at 4,224 feet (1,287 m), is the highest point the road reaches in Virginia.

Once across the North Carolina state line, however, the Blue Ridge Parkway shows a very different side of itself, taking you to the higher, wilder-looking Great Smoky Mountains, with the road climbing well above 6,000 feet (1,830 m) in places. Dramatic gorges, waterfalls, and a succession of long, dark tunnels worming through the mountains add to the sense of adventure.

ALTERNATE ROUTE

For those who want even more of a great thing, the equally beautiful Skyline Drive offers a 105-mile (169 km) continuation through Shenandoah National Park. Starting at the northern terminus of the Blue Ridge Parkway, it winds through the mountains with 75 scenic lookout points—and more than 11,000 feet (3,355 m) of climbing—on its way to Afton, Virginia. Skyline Drive was largely built during the Great Depression by the Civilian Conservation Corps. It was designated a national landmark in 2008.

SAN JUAN ISLANDS

Island-hop by ferry and bicycle around Washington's postcard-pretty Puget Sound.

DISTANCE: 40 to 80 miles (64 to 129 km)   **SURFACE: Paved**   **LENGTH OF TRIP: 3 days**
WHEN TO GO: Summer   **DIFFICULTY: Moderate**

Tucked away in the sheltered waters of Washington's Puget Sound, the beautiful, laid-back San Juan Islands are perfect for exploring by bicycle—a lyrical blend of lighthouses, fishing villages, vineyards, and lavender farms on a rolling landscape with scenic viewpoints offering the possibility of spotting a pod of orcas playing in the sound.

The three main islands in the archipelago—San Juan, Lopez, and Orcas—offer very different cycling experiences, and because they are linked by ferries, you can island-hop and explore all three at your leisure. Lopez Island is the least hilly of them. A 31-mile (50 km) loop of the island on its quiet roads lets you take in a mix of farmlands, marshlands, and hedgerows that exude a curiously English feel—aside from the long views over Puget Sound with the snowcapped Olympic Mountains forming a backdrop.

San Juan Island is larger and hillier, and its main town, Friday Harbor (pop. 2,587), is the biggest settlement on the islands. Here you'll ride through a landscape of vineyards, lavender farms, and rocky coves—and by the historic lighthouse at Lime Kiln Point State Park, which is also one of the best places for whale-spotting.

Orcas Island is rustic and hilly, with narrow roads and steep grades and the challenge of pedaling to the top of Mount Constitution, the highest point in the archipelago at 2,409 feet (734 m), with breathtaking views of Puget Sound.

TOP TIP: Catch the ferry out to the islands from Anacortes, about 79 miles (127 km) north of Seattle.

OPPOSITE: **A cyclist pauses to take in the view in Moran State Park on Orcas Island, one of the San Juan Islands.**

GOING-TO-THE-SUN ROAD

Often touted as the most beautiful road in America, this serpentine ascent in Glacier National Park is at its very best in spring.

DISTANCE: 64 miles (103 km) **SURFACE: Paved** **LENGTH OF TRIP: I day**
WHEN TO GO: Late May, before the road opens to motor traffic **DIFFICULTY: Challenging**

Ascending more than 3,000 feet (915 m) through deep forests and alpine meadows, with glacial-carved peaks towering all around, long views of cascading waterfalls, and banks of wildflowers rioting along the roadside, Going-to-the-Sun Road is one of America's most spectacular drives. Built during the 1920s to give tourists access to some of Glacier National Park's more remote beauty spots, the Sun Road, as it's sometimes called, stretches 50 miles (80 km) through the heart of the park, climbing up and over the Continental Divide at Logan Pass. It has become so famous and popular that motorists wishing to drive the road during the brief, busy summer season need to book ahead for a permit.

While cyclists don't need a permit even in summer, the real magic for them happens late in the spring, during those few glorious weeks before the road is officially open to motor traffic, when cyclists have this stunning drive all to themselves.

Heavy snows close the road during the winter months, with drifts as high as 80 feet (24 m) on the eastern flank of Logan Pass. Snow-clearing operations start in April, and usually by early May the lower parts of the road are open to cyclists. Thereafter, as the plows progress higher up the pass, more of the road is opened behind them—not to motorists, only cyclists and hikers.

OPPOSITE: Going-to-the-Sun Road stretches through Glacier National Park.

PAGES 102-3: Ascending Going-to-the-Sun Road with snowcapped mountains in the distance

By early June it is often possible to pedal from the park's western entrance all the way to the top of Logan Pass—a spectacular 64-mile (103 km) out-and-back ride, and all of it traffic free.

It's an easy ride for the first few miles, a serpentine run through tall forest along Lake McDonald and upstream along McDonald Creek. The real adventure—and the climbing—begins at Avalanche Campground, about 15 miles (24 km) into the ride. From here the road ramps up at a steady rate of about 7 percent, which is not a brutal gradient but enough to keep you warm in the chilly mountain air. If you find the pedaling hard going, imagine having to build this road—the work crews back in the 1920s had to hike up here each day, and often had to work roped up as they carved the road into cliffs on the hillsides. Small wonder that the turnover in the workforce was 300 percent in the early months of the project.

Soon you come to the Loop. It may be the only switchback on the climb, but it's a spectacular one,

CYCLING THROUGH HISTORY

In 1910, when Glacier became America's 10th national park, much of its beauty was inaccessible to ordinary people. So Congress approved a plan in 1921 to build a single scenic road across the park, a task that turned out to be extremely challenging, with surveyors dangling on ropes from cliff faces as they laid out the road, and workmen having to trudge 3,000 feet (914 m) up into the mountains each day. The road opened in July 1933, with a fleet of red buses taking tourists through the park. Restored versions of these buses make the same run today.

ABOVE: Pause to take in the scenery from Cave Lookout on the Going-to-the-Sun Road path.

OPPOSITE: The spring snow-melt makes for slippery conditions.

with the road doubling back sharply on itself and offering a stunning view of 8,987-foot (2,739 m) Heaven's Peak. Highlights to come include a thundering cataract called Bird Woman Falls and the spectacular displays of wildflowers on a distant rocky ridge known as the Garden Wall. The climb tops out at the crest of 6,646-foot (2,026 m) Logan Pass. Later in the season, when the eastern flank of the pass is finally cleared of its immense snowdrifts, you'll be able to ride down the other side, an 18-mile (29 km) glide to the park's eastern entrance, but later in the year there will be traffic. Until then, it's one of the world's most amazing cycle paths.

TOP TIPS: Remember to pack a jacket and prepare for a chilly descent. Another thing to remember is bear spray. There may be no motor traffic this time of year, but the park's grizzly bears are coming out of hibernation and often stroll along the newly cleared road.

CABOT TRAIL

Explore the rugged coastlines, forests, and heather-clad highlands of Maritime Canada's Cape Breton Island.

DISTANCE: **186 miles (299 km)**   SURFACE: **Paved**   LENGTH OF TRIP: **3 to 5 days**
WHEN TO GO: **Summer**   DIFFICULTY: **Challenging**

Nova Scotia is said to be one of the world's most beautiful islands, and this 186-mile (299 km) loop takes in the best of what this gorgeous Maritime Province has to offer: rocky coastlines, old-growth forests, heather-draped highlands, secluded coves, and picturesque fishing villages tucked away in a wilderness setting that feels pleasantly removed from the rest of the world.

Named for the Italian explorer John Cabot, who visited the island in 1497, the Cabot Trail is not actually a trail but rather a public road that was built in 1932 to link the isolated fishing villages on Cape Breton Island. Four years after the road was laid out, the nation set aside 366 square miles (948 sq km) of wilderness at the northern end of the cape as Cape Breton Highlands National Park, forming a wild and rugged backdrop for what would become a world-famous drive and cycling route. More than a third of the Cabot Trail passes through the national park, with the rest hugging the dramatic and unspoiled Atlantic coastline.

Whether you ride the loop in a clockwise or counterclockwise direction is a matter of personal preference. Each has its advantages. If you ride counterclockwise, you'll always be on the side of the road nearest the sea and enjoy better views from the saddle, while a clockwise ride is said to offer better shelter from the winds, which can be strong and consistent out here, as well as slightly easier approaches up some of the steeper hills. Whichever way you choose, the riding is rich and varied, taking in some of Canada's most

OPPOSITE: **The cliffside views are worth the trek on the Cabot Trail.**

PAGES 108-9: **Stop in Baddeck for a photo op with a statue of inventor Alexander Graham Bell and his wife, Mabel Bell.**

beautiful scenery. Encounters with moose and bears are possible in the woodlands.

Although the terrain is generally undulating, there are some challenging bits, with gradients on the climbs up Smokey Mountain (1,200 feet/ 366 meters) and North Mountain (1,460 feet/ 445 meters) reaching up to 15 percent. The six-mile (9.6 km) climb from Ingonish Harbour up the flanks of Smokey Mountain (traveling clockwise) is especially memorable. French Mountain (1,492 feet/ 455 meters) is the literal high point on the trail.

Since the Cabot Trail is a loop, one can begin anywhere, but most cyclists start their rides at Baddeck along the shores of Bras d'Or Lake, where Alexander Graham Bell had his summer retreat. It offers the easiest access from Sydney or Halifax. Nova Scotia is remote, and getting there takes time and planning, but then if it were easier to get to, everybody would do it. September is the optimum time to go. The mornings are chillier, but the road is less trafficked, the mosquitoes have disappeared, and the autumn foliage is out in all its glory.

REST STOP

Cape Breton has a vibrant tradition of Scots-Gaelic culture, a legacy dating back to the Highland Clearances of the late 18th century, when many Scots were forced off their ancestral lands by British government decree. Thousands settled in Nova Scotia (New Scotland). The Gaelic College was founded in 1938 to preserve and promote the Gaelic language, music, and crafts. Located in St. Ann's along the Cabot Trail, it makes for an interesting stop along the way.

GREENBRIER RIVER TRAIL

A free and easy adventure through the wilds of West Virginia

DISTANCE: 78 miles (126 km)   **SURFACE:** Crushed gravel   **LENGTH OF TRIP:** 1 to 2 days
WHEN TO GO: Spring through autumn   **DIFFICULTY:** Easy

There can be no better initiation to the joys of remote bicycle touring than this scenic rails-to-trails offering in the wilds of West Virginia. Following the tracks of an old Chesapeake & Ohio Railway line, abandoned in 1978, the Greenbrier River Trail runs along the banks of the Greenbrier River between the towns of Cass and Caldwell, through some of the most remote parts of the state. At nearly 80 miles (129 km) in length, it is the longest rails-to-trails path in West Virginia, and by many reckonings one of the most beautiful on the entire rails-to-trails network.

The trail offers more than just the rustic scenery of an old Appalachian river valley—it's accessible adventure, for this is a genuinely remote ride. Only one town of any size lies along it—Marlinton—so riders have to come prepared and be reasonably self-sufficient. That said, there are campgrounds every eight to 10 miles (13 to 16 km). And with a smooth riding surface and an average gradient of one percent or less, the pedaling couldn't be easier. Start at the northern end at Cass Scenic Railroad State Park and follow the river downstream. As you wend your way along the valley floor, you pass a few old Appalachian hamlets, cross the river several times on antique railroad bridges, and pass through two tunnels—the Droop Mountain Tunnel, built in 1900, and the Sharps Tunnel, built in 1899—all of which add to the sense of adventure along the trail.

OPPOSITE: **A bridge on the Greenbrier River Trail in West Virginia**

MAUNA KEA

Test your cycling mettle from surf to summit on the world's toughest and most spectacular climb.

DISTANCE: 55 miles (89 km)   **SURFACE:** Mostly paved, stretches of loose gravel   **LENGTH OF TRIP:** 1 day
WHEN TO GO: Year-round (it's Hawaii)   **DIFFICULTY:** Extreme

Here it is: the big kahuna—the most brutal cycling climb on the face of the planet, bar none. Don't fool yourself. Nothing about this one is easy. The toughest cols on the Tour de France are molehills in comparison. But for bragging rights, saying you pedaled to the summit of Mauna Kea pretty well guarantees you the floor.

Simply put, Hawaii's volcanic Mauna Kea is the world's biggest mountain, towering some 33,500 feet (10,200 m) above its base on the ocean floor. Of that, some 13,796 feet (4,205 m) rise directly above the sea in one stunning sweep to the summit. For sheer vertical relief, and with a road running right to the top, there is no greater cycling challenge for those who like to conquer hills.

The route starts in warm tropical sunshine beside the sea and finishes up 55 switchback miles (89 km) later in the chilly, bleak moonscape and razor-thin air high above sea level, with a sea of clouds spreading below. The climb is relentless: a 14-mile (23 km) stretch averaging 9 percent; an eight-mile (13 km) stretch averaging 12 percent; an "easy" segment of 10 miles (16 km) where the gradient is "only" 7 percent—which on its own is as tough as some of the *hors catégorie* (the most difficult) climbs in the Tour de France. And saving best for last: the final nasty pitch to the summit, along a loose gravel road with long gradients in excess of 20 percent.

Beginning from Waikoloa Beach, where it's tradition to dip your rear wheel into the sea before your ascent, the route is fairly tame for the first few miles—uphill, of course, but at a relatively easy pitch, although heat and humidity

ALTERNATE ROUTE

If Hawaii is too far afield, there's always Pikes Peak, the 14,115-foot (4,302 m) summit in the Colorado Rockies. Today a paved road runs to the summit. It may not be as tough as the Mauna Kea climb, but it is plenty challenging, with grades averaging 7 percent, nearly 5,000 feet (1,525 m) of vertical elevation gain, and more than 150 switchback curves.

OPPOSITE: The volcanic cones of Mauna Kea

PAGES 114-15: Ascending Mauna Kea amid the clouds

and the trade winds can make even this a challenge. It's when you reach Old Saddle Road that the climbing starts. Still on good tarmac, it takes you up to the turnoff to Mauna Kea Access Road, at about 6,588 feet (2,008 m). You'll find the air noticeably cooler and, having just left sea level, thinner as well. Already you've pedaled up the equivalent of some of the highest, hardest cols in the Alps, but you're not even halfway to the summit. In terms of this monster climb, you've only done the warm-up.

From here the climb really ramps up as the road ascends toward the Maunakea Visitor Information Station at more than 9,000 feet (2,745 m). All of it is steep, but on one particularly tough two-mile (3.2 km) stretch the gradient *averages* 13 percent. By the time you wobble into the parking lot at the information station, not only are your leg muscles feeling like jelly but the altitude is taking a toll as well. You're already higher than the highest paved pass in the Alps, but you still have another 4,000-plus feet (1,220 m) of elevation gain to reach the summit—and what comes next is the toughest part of the climb.

CYCLING THROUGH HISTORY

To native Hawaiians, the summit of Mauna Kea is a place of profound spiritual significance. The mountain is named after Wakea, the Polynesian god of the sky who married Papahanaumoku, the Earth goddess. The presence of a series of astronomical observatories on the summit has been controversial, with some seeing similarities with the way early Hawaiians explored the heavens, and others seeing the construction on the summit as a desecration.

ABOVE: The Pacific greets the rocky volcanic coast with Mauna Kea in the distance.

OPPOSITE: Catch your breath after the ascent near the Maunakea Observatories.

The next four and a half miles (7.2 km) are on loose gravel and dusty volcanic ash, with road gradients in excess of 20 percent. Motorists are warned that it is four-wheel drive only from here to the top. Cyclists will find their skinny tires sinking and slithering in stretches of deep, soft ash. Some sections simply must be walked, but even walking while pushing a bike up the grade is a challenge at this altitude.

The gravel section ends at about 12,000 feet (3,660 m), still with nearly 2,000 feet (610 m) of elevation gain to go. These last four miles (6.4 km) take forever, pedaling endlessly upward through what looks and feels like a moonscape, until at last the observatory comes into view. You've made it, and earned some serious bragging rights for tackling the highest, toughest hill climb on the planet.

VÉLOROUTE DES BLEUETS

A sparkling lake, steepled villages, and blueberry bogs highlight this hidden gem of a ride off the beaten track in rural Québec.

DISTANCE: 160 miles (257 km)   SURFACE: Paved   LENGTH OF TRIP: 3 to 5 days
WHEN TO GO: Late July through August (blueberry season)   DIFFICULTY: Easy

Tucked away in the wilds of Québec, the Véloroute des Bleuets (Blueberry Bicycle Route) loop around sparkling Saguenay-Lac-Saint-Jean is named for the blueberries that grow in such profusion here. The starting point is the town of Alma, about a two-hour drive north of Québec City, where the lake flows into the Saguenay River.

Set out into a gently rolling countryside of farmland, forests, and blueberry bogs. Charming villages and towns along the way offer local cheeses, beers from microbreweries, and all sorts of blueberry goodies: pies, jams, cakes, syrups, and more. Highlights include Pointe-Taillon National Park, a wooded peninsula that juts into the lake, and masses of wild blueberries ripe for the picking. If you like, veer off the official route at the park and pedal another eight miles (12.9 km) out to the tip of the peninsula—just take a short ferry ride to Péribonka, where you can rejoin the trail and continue your journey around the lake.

The trail itself is an easy-to-follow mix of dedicated bicycle paths, quiet country lanes, and the paved shoulders of larger roads. Towns are bicycle-friendly, and local outfitters rent bicycles—including e-bikes—and can organize tours. After your loop of the lake, you can keep right on going—another 200 miles (322 km) along the hillier but equally lovely Véloroute du Fjord du Saguenay.

BREAKOUT

Both Véloroute des Bleuets and Véloroute du Fjord du Saguenay are part of Québec's glorious Route Verte, the largest network of bicycle routes in North America, at more than 3,000 miles (4,830 km)—and growing. For more information, see *routeverte.com*.

OPPOSITE: Québec's sun-dappled Véloroute des Bleuets (Blueberry Bicycle Route)

WHITE RIM TRAIL

Rugged adventure in the remote red-rock country of outback Utah

DISTANCE: **103 miles (166 km)**   SURFACE: **Gravel**   LENGTH OF TRIP: **1 to 3 days**
WHEN TO GO: **Spring or autumn**   DIFFICULTY: **Challenging**

Staggeringly beautiful, wild, and remote, Utah's White Rim Trail makes a 103-mile (166 km) loop around the Island in the Sky mesa, nestled between the Colorado and Green Rivers in Canyonlands National Park, about a 30-mile (48 km) drive from the world-famous mountain biking hot spot of Moab.

Though not a technically difficult route—it is essentially a jeep track, albeit a rugged one—White Rim's remoteness and harsh desert environment, and the need for endurance and self-sufficiency, make doing it without a support vehicle a serious challenge. Even with a support vehicle this is not a ride to be taken lightly. But the rewards—the haunting silences, the ancient red landscapes and eerie rock formations, the sky ablaze with stars at night— make this ride worth every crank of the pedals.

Many riders begin by descending the Shafer Trail, in the eastern side of the park, and riding the loop clockwise. You certainly get off to a flying start this way—a precipitous 1,400-foot (427 m) plunge down a series of exhilarating switchbacks that take you down to the bottom of the plateau and onto the 280-million-year-old White Rim sandstone formation for which the trail is named.

You're committed now. This is where you join White Rim Road, a jeep track originally built by the Atomic Energy Commission during the Cold War days of the 1950s to provide access for uranium prospectors who were searching for the stuff to make atom bombs. But there was not as much uranium out here as the government had initially hoped, and mines were abandoned

OPPOSITE: Jutting cliffs make for a scenic—and intimidating—path on the White Rim Trail.

PAGES 122-23: Friends gather for some R&R under an expansive night sky at the Airport campsite.

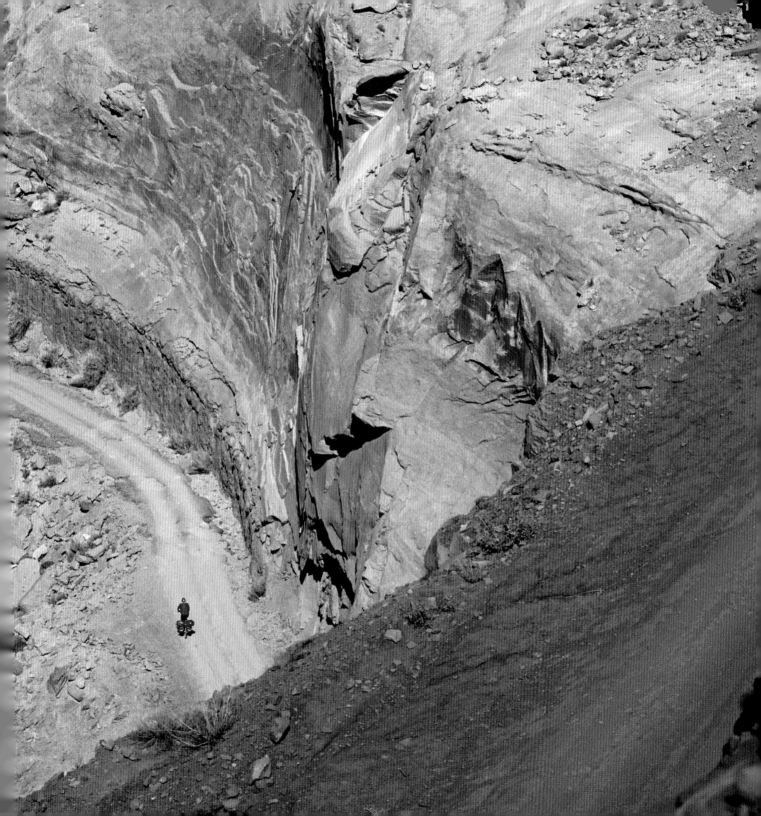

long ago, leaving a jeep track for posterity (and 21st-century mountain bikers). The track meanders through a rugged landscape of junipers and cacti and a geological wonderland of red-rock cliffs, spires, arches, precipices, canyons, and mesas. Every turn and rise brings a new and astonishing view, a fresh take on the Colorado River, perhaps, or glimpses of bighorn sheep perched precariously on a cliff face.

At about the halfway point on your ride, you'll find yourself pedaling up Murphy Hogback, one of the steepest climbs on the route. A swift descent awaits on the other side, followed by miles of rolling desert terrain along the Green River before the final two climbs: Hardscrabble Hill, which is nearly as tough as Murphy Hogback, and the somewhat easier Horsethief Trail, which brings you back up onto the plateau where your adventure began.

KNOW BEFORE YOU GO

Planning is crucial if you want to tackle the White Rim Trail. There is no potable drinking water anywhere along the route. You must carry every drop you need. The National Park Service recommends one gallon (3.7 L) per person per day; so for a three-day trip, you'll start off carrying more than 25 pounds (11 kg) in water weight alone. A support vehicle makes carrying supplies that much easier, but bear in mind that White Rim Road is no place for a novice in a four-wheel drive. Getting a vehicle stuck out here can be very, very expensive.

LA CARRETERA DE LOS YUNGAS

Hairpin curves, crumbling cliff edges, a 15,400-foot (4,694 m) descent, and serious bragging rights await the intrepid on the world's scariest mountain road.

DISTANCE: **43 miles (69 km)**   SURFACE: **Gravel**   LENGTH OF TRIP: **1 day**
WHEN TO GO: **June through August (dry season)**   DIFFICULTY: **Extreme**

Once famed as the world's most dangerous road, Bolivia's notorious Carretera de los Yungas makes a harrowing descent down a 15,400-foot (4,694 m) pass in the Andes to steamy, jungle-clad lowlands on the other side. In the bad old days when this was a major truck route, this terrifying stretch of road—nicknamed the Bolivian Death Road—reputedly claimed a few hundred lives a year. Unpaved, with sheer cliffs, plunging precipices, and hairpin curves with no guardrails, it was almost cartoonishly scary.

Thankfully, a new paved road offers a much safer route over the pass, while the old Death Road is enjoying a colorful retirement as one of the world's great mountain bike descents. A number of mountain bike outfitters in La Paz offer intrepid cyclists a chance to experience the Death Road's heart-stopping curves and 2,000-foot (610 m) drop-offs and enjoy bragging rights whenever the talk turns to risky roads.

The journey starts with an hour-long bus ride from La Paz to La Cumbre—the summit—the crest of the pass where the Death Road begins its white-knuckle descent to the town of Coroico. It's a harrowing descent, but the views into the lowland jungles are incredible. You can always bail out and ride down in the support van with no loss of face, or, if you're really feeling your oats, turn around at the bottom and ride back up.

OPPOSITE: **Clouds cloak a winding stretch of the "world's most dangerous road" down to Coroico in the Yungas.**

MOUNTAIN HERO

Part of an award-winning network of MTB trails laid
out by Canada's First Nations people

DISTANCE: **18 miles (29 km)**   SURFACE: **Off-road track**   LENGTH OF TRIP: **I day**
WHEN TO GO: **Summer through autumn**   DIFFICULTY: **Challenging**

C anada's remote Yukon is fast becoming one of the world's great
mountain biking hot spots, with hundreds of miles of glorious
singletrack crisscrossing the wilderness landscapes, and the midnight sun in summer offering 24-hour daylight for riding.

One of the very best of these trails is Mountain Hero, an 18-mile (29 km)
loop that has been rated an "Epic" ride by the International Mountain Biking
Association. It's part of a larger network of mountain bike trails developed
by the Tagish First Nations people in the Singletrack to Success project, an
initiative that began in 2006 to help local youths connect with their ancestral
lands. Working with community leaders, teenagers learn how to design and
maintain trails, protect heritage sites, identify plants and trees, and learn
traditional place-names. The result has been an incredible 47-mile (76 km)
network of award-winning MTB trails that now draw enthusiastic riders from
all over the world.

The origins of the Mountain Hero trail date back to silver mining days
around 1905, when the path was a mule track used to haul supplies up the
mountain for the construction of the Mountain Hero tramway, which itself
was built to service the silver mine.

Fans of Canada's "Bard of the Yukon," Robert Service, will appreciate that

OPPOSITE: **A pair of mountain bikers battle the singletrack in Carcross, Yukon.**

PAGES 128-29: **The Mountain
Hero trail is part of a network that extends through
400 miles (645 km) of
remote wilderness in the
rugged Yukon.**

the original early 20th-century path was supposedly laid out by the legendary Sam McGee, whose fictionalized cremation was celebrated in verse by the British Canadian poet in "The Cremation of Sam McGee." The real-life Sam McGee was a well-known roadbuilder in the Yukon who died—in much less colorful circumstances—of a heart attack at his daughter's farm in Alberta in 1940. His surname just happened to suit the rhyme Service had in mind when he was writing a poem about a real-life cremation that happened elsewhere in the Yukon.

The Mountain Hero route starts off with a long ascent through boreal forest up to breezy subalpine highlands, where your hard work is rewarded with stunning 360-degree views of the endless wilderness spreading out around you.

From this point on, it's a fast, flowy descent along brilliant singletrack following an alpine ridge, with another small climb to go before the plunge back down into the tree line and on to the shores of Nares Lake, a spring migration area for thousands of waterfowl. Closing the loop on the way back to town adds another few miles to the ride. If you prefer, you can arrange a shuttle. Carcross (originally dubbed Caribou Crossing due to the animals' migration path through the town

ABOVE: Vintage tools highlight the gold rush history of the Yukon.

OPPOSITE: Mountain bikers take on the amazing single-track in Carcross.

and surrounding region) is about an hour's drive south of the territory's capital of Whitehorse, which has become a must-go mountain biking destination of its own. With more than 400 miles (645 km) of wilderness trails in the immediate vicinity of the city and a population of less than 30,000, you won't be running into crowds.

Spare a few minutes during your trip to visit the sandy dunes of Carcross Desert, known as the "world's smallest desert" at just one square mile (2.6 sq km). Though not technically a desert by classical definition, the dunes are still a sight to see, nestled at the foot of the craggy mountains and dusted with a fine powder of snow.

MOUNT TAM

An iconic ride into the hills above San Francisco with a sweeping panorama from the top

DISTANCE: **19 miles (30 km)**   SURFACE: **Paved public road**   LENGTH OF TRIP: **1 day**
WHEN TO GO: **Year-round**   DIFFICULTY: **Challenging**

Among mountain bikers, Mount Tamalpais Old Railroad Grade Trail—"Mount Tam" in the vernacular—has long been a name that conjures some magic. Back in the 1970s it was on Mount Tam's steep single-track that mountain biking pioneers such as Gary Fisher, Otis Guy, and Joe Breeze popularized the idea of adrenaline-pumping off-road adventure.

Mount Tam is still a honeypot for mountain bikers, but it also has plenty to offer roadies and gravel bikers, with glorious climbs ascending through the redwoods to its 2,571-foot (784 m) East Peak and its sweeping panoramas of San Francisco.

Two of the best routes up the mountain start from Mill Valley, a town about 14 miles (23 km) north of San Francisco.

Start at Depot Plaza, once the terminus of the Mount Tamalpais Scenic Railway, which opened in 1896. (Among its first passengers was suffragist Susan B. Anthony.) Pedal east out of town until you come to the trailhead of the Old Railroad Grade Trail. With 281 curves and switchbacks and 22 trestles, this was known as "the crookedest railway in the world."

After a steady climb through a redwood forest and a series of tight switch-backs, you break out of the woods and can start enjoying the distant views of the bay. About two-thirds of the way up the mountain you come to quaint, old West Point Inn, which opened in 1904 and is today run by volunteers.

The descent from Mount Tam is pure joy, an exhilarating 11-mile (18 km) spin on smooth, curvy bitumen that brings you back to Depot Plaza, where the day's adventures began.

ARMCHAIR RIDE

In *Around the World on a Bicycle* (1887), Thomas Stevens sets off from San Francisco in 1884, bound for Boston aboard a 50-inch (127 cm) Columbia penny-farthing—packing only a spare shirt, an oilskin slicker, and a bulldog revolver—to become the first per-son to circle the globe on a bicycle.

OPPOSITE: A curving descent in Mount Tamalpais State Park

THE KATY TRAIL

Follow in the footsteps of Lewis and Clark traffic free along America's single longest rails-to-trails cycling path.

DISTANCE: **239 miles (385 km)**   SURFACE: **Crushed rock**   LENGTH OF TRIP: **1 week**
WHEN TO GO: **Autumn**   DIFFICULTY: **Easy**

Built on the corridor of the former Missouri-Kansas-Texas Railroad—aka the K-T ("Katy") Line—this gentle route offers 239 miles (385 km) of nearly level, traffic-free cycling on a smooth crushed-gravel path that leads you through shifting landscapes of farmlands, vineyards, forests, and prairies, with the bighearted Missouri River as your riding companion for much of the way.

Since it's a point-to-point path, you can start the Katy Trail in either direction. Some prefer traveling west to east, on the theory that you'll be riding with the prevailing winds. Others prefer the idea of venturing west, as the pioneers did and, before them, the explorers Lewis and Clark, whose 1805 expedition followed roughly the same route as the Katy Trail through the heart of Missouri.

As for the old railway mileposts, they run east to west, with milepost zero in St. Louis at what was the eastern terminus of the line.

Officially at least, the Katy Trail begins at a rather hard-to-find trailhead at milepost 26, near the small town of Machens. Most riders begin in nearby picturesque St. Charles (milepost 39), where the trail runs through town, by the old railway depot. St. Charles was Missouri's original state capital, and with its historic district and cobbled streets, bike shops, cafés, and boutique B&Bs, it makes for a genteel springboard for a genteel ride.

St. Charles is where Lewis and Clark set off on their expedition; there is a statue of them in town. You'll find the going much easier than they did as

OPPOSITE: Vineyards are a scenic backdrop to the Katy Trail.

PAGES 136-37: A section of the Katy Trail near Rocheport, Missouri, follows alongside the Missouri River.

you head west along a smooth ribbon of finely packed gravel that shadows the Missouri River through more than 40 towns, over old railway truss bridges, and, as you go farther west, along spectacular limestone bluffs where the river carved its course millions of years ago.

Along the way, you'll also find yourself passing through miles of wine country. The town of Hermann (milepost 101), founded in 1847 by German immigrants, was once one of the world's top wine-growing regions, with its vintages winning gold medals in international wine shows. Its pest-resistant rootstock helped save the French wine industry after a global insect infestation killed off much of the world's grapevines in the late 19th century. Prohibition put an end to Missouri's wine industry, but since the 1980s it has bounced back with a vengeance. Wine tastings, vineyard tours, and the quality restaurants that tend to pop up in wine districts are a feature of this ride. Go in autumn, after the summer heat and humidity have passed. Hermann also puts on a great Oktoberfest.

CYCLING THROUGH HISTORY

Back in 1896, the Katy achieved worldwide fame when it staged a head-on collision between two speeding locomotives as a publicity stunt a little farther down the line in Texas. The locomotives slammed into each other at 45 miles an hour (72 km/h). Both boilers exploded, killing two spectators and seriously injuring several others. Ragtime composer Scott Joplin even wrote a song about it: "The Great Crush Collision March."

COLORADO TRAIL

A full-scale wilderness bikepacking expedition in the Colorado high country

DISTANCE: **567 miles (912 km)**   SURFACE: **Mixed; 80 percent unpaved, 55 percent singletrack**
LENGTH OF TRIP: **1 to 3 weeks**   WHEN TO GO: **Summer**   DIFFICULTY: **Extreme**

For a few glorious weeks each summer, the Colorado Rockies high alpine passes are sufficiently clear of snow for intrepid bikepackers to ride the Colorado Trail, one of the grandest high-altitude wilderness adventures you can have on a bicycle.

Starting in Littleton, on the outskirts of Denver, the trail passes through eight mountain ranges and six national forests on its way to Durango, in the state's southwest. A handful of quirky Old West mining towns and ski villages provide chances to take a breather and restock your supplies along the way, but much of this trail passes through extremely remote country at high altitude. And the going is tough, involving more than 72,000 feet (21,945 m) of elevation gain with occasional sections of what wilderness bikepackers call "hike-a-bike": bits of the trail that are simply too rough to be ridden. Bear spray and bug spray are essential. And with much of the trail above the tree line—the average elevation on the Colorado Trail is more than 10,000 feet (3,050 m), rising to 13,000 (3,962 m) in places—weather plays a big role, with violent summer thunderstorms adding to the drama and danger. But for the well prepared, the miles of endlessly evolving alpine scenery, free-flowing singletrack, and exhilarating remoteness make this a very special ride.

You can begin the ride at either end, but a Littleton start eases you into the high country, giving you time to acclimatize, and saves the remoter and most spectacular stretches for later. The descent into Durango is magic.

TOP TIP: The *Colorado Trail Databook* contains essential information and is worth its weight in your saddlebag.

OPPOSITE: **A cyclist makes a splash in the high alpine mountain region of the Colorado Trail outside Durango, Colorado.**

NASHVILLE, TENNESSEE, TO NATCHEZ, MISSISSIPPI, U.S.A.

NATCHEZ TRACE PARKWAY

Spin along a sleepy backwoods highway through the heart of America's Deep South.

DISTANCE: **444 miles (715 km)**   SURFACE: **Paved public road**   LENGTH OF TRIP: **7 to 10 days**
WHEN TO GO: **May through June or September through October**   DIFFICULTY: **Easy to moderate**

As smooth as a mint julep, the Natchez Trace Parkway flows some 444 miles (715 km) through the center of America's Deep South, starting in Nashville, Tennessee, and ending in the gracious antebellum riverboat town of Natchez, once known as the Jewel of the Mississippi. Along the way, it passes through the wooded hills and drowsy farmlands of Alabama and Mississippi. Side trails offer access to attractions from Civil War battlefields and a memorial to the explorer Meriwether Lewis, who died along the trace in 1809, to Elvis Presley's humble birthplace in Tupelo, Mississippi.

One sight you *won't* see along this ribbon of highway are stop signs or billboards or truck traffic—or much traffic of any sort. This is a beautifully quiet road. The National Park Service has designated the entire parkway a bike route, with plenty of signs advising motorists that cyclists are on the road, and the speed limit is restricted to 50 miles an hour (80 km/h). That said, as a cyclist, you should still do your part: Ride courteously, be visible, and exercise caution where the parkway passes near population centers such as Tupelo, especially during peak commuting times.

It's an easy-to-pedal route, gently rolling, with most of the steeper hills at the Tennessee end flattening out as you head south. The modern parkway

OPPOSITE: Wildflowers, lush forests, and meandering curves provide a relaxing landscape in which to cycle through history.

PAGES 142–43: A biker studies a civil rights mural in Port Gibson, Mississippi.

follows the path of the Old Natchez Trace, a woodland hunting trail used for thousands of years by the ancestors of the Choctaw and Chickasaw peoples.

By the early years of the 19th century, the ancient path had been widened by the U.S. Army and was used by settlers from the Ohio Valley, who would float their produce on rafts down the Ohio and Mississippi Rivers to Natchez, sell everything—including the raft—and then hike the almost 450 miles (725 km) back home along the trace, which by then was quickly acquiring a reputation as a rough and dangerous road infested with bandits. The advent of the steamboat era put an end to the trace's days, with travelers much preferring the safety of coming and going by riverboat to the hardships and dangers of life on the road.

Jump forward two centuries, and hardships along the Natchez Trace are few and the only

CYCLING THROUGH HISTORY

Although the finishing touches to the Natchez Trace Parkway were completed as recently as 2005, the original pathway has been used for thousands of years and is rich in Native American archaeology. One of the most spectacular sites along the route is Emerald Mound, a mysterious earthen mound dating back to the 13th century that was apparently used for ceremonial purposes during what archaeologists refer to as the Mississippian period of prehistory. It was abandoned by the 1600s. Located near Natchez, it is a national historic landmark today.

bandits you're likely to encounter are nosy raccoons looking to help themselves to whatever food you may have unwisely left in your panniers overnight. This is still very much a backwoods route. While camping opportunities abound along the parkway—campsites are free, with five campgrounds designated exclusively for cyclists—you need to plan ahead if you want a roof over your head at night or to stay in some of the historic B&Bs in towns near the trail, and likewise for replenishing your food and water supplies along the way. With few access points and laws prohibiting advertising signage along the rustic road, you need to know where you're going. Happily, the Park Service provides a list of places to eat and buy groceries along the fabled parkway. Spring and autumn are the best seasons to do this trip, avoiding the heat and humidity of midsummer and giving you the much more pleasant choice of dogwoods in bloom (spring) or glorious foliage (autumn).

ABOVE: A colorful guitar marks the entrance to the Elvis Presley Birthplace Museum and Chapel.

OPPOSITE: A verdant cypress swamp along the Natchez Trace Parkway north of Jackson, Mississippi

CARRETERA AUSTRAL

Step away from it all along one of South America's most beautiful and remote highways.

DISTANCE: **770 miles (1,239 km)**   SURFACE: **Mixed; paved and unpaved public roads**
LENGTH OF TRIP: **3 to 4 weeks**   WHEN TO GO: **October through April**   DIFFICULTY: **Moderate to challenging**

"Those who hurry through Patagonia waste their time." So goes a proud Chilean saying, and never could it be better applied than to a journey along this iconic Patagonian road. Starting in the picturesque old seaport of Puerto Montt in the southern part of Chile, the Carretera Austral (Southern Highway) rolls south through hauntingly remote landscapes of fjords and forests, turquoise lakes and glacier-carved mountains, to the Patagonian town of Villa O'Higgins, 770 miles (1,239 km) away. The month or so it takes to pedal its length is time well spent indeed, which is why this jewel of a ride ranks high on the bucket lists of the world's touring cyclists.

The highway itself is fairly new. Work started on it under the Augusto Pinochet regime in 1976, the idea being to link the isolated communities in Chile's far south, which until then could be reached only by boat or packhorse, and also to fly the flag and demonstrate Chilean sovereignty over the region at a time when relations with neighboring Argentina were strained. Politics changed over the decades, but not the remoteness of the landscape or the challenges of building a highway through it. The final 60 miles (97 km) of the Carretera Austral weren't completed until 2003. Even today much of it remains unpaved.

OPPOSITE: **The stunning Cuevas de Mármol (Marble Caves) of General Carrera Lake in northern Patagonia, Chile**

PAGES 148-49: **A cyclist ascends a hill on the Carretera Austral in southern Patagonia, Chile.**

Cycling the Carretera Austral is fairly simple—just get on it and go. There's only this one lonely ribbon of highway stretching from Puerto Montt. As you make your way south, the scenery becomes more and more spectacular—a rush of waterfalls, wildflowers, mountains, lakes, and fjords.

The whole of the ride has a remote wilderness feel, but among the highlights are Pumalín National Park, a vast tract of ancient temperate rainforest, and, not far away, the three-mile (5 km) round-trip hiking trail up the flanks of Chaitén volcano. Farther south is Queulat National Park, with its hanging glacier and frozen waterfalls, and beyond that Parque Cerro Castillo, with its pristine lakes and forests of antarctic beech. From here on, the road is mainly gravel.

The final stop on the route is one of the remotest towns in Chile: Villa O'Higgins, named for the early 19th-century Chilean independence leader Bernardo O'Higgins. Surrounded by glacier-clad mountains and accessed by ferry across a vast lake, it is a fitting end to a cycle trip along one of South America's most remarkable highways.

ALTERNATE ROUTE

Although the Carretera Austral ends in Villa O'Higgins, intrepid cyclists can push on another 40 circuitous miles (64 km) and cross the border into Argentina by taking a combination of backroads, a very rugged three-mile (4.8 km) hiking path, and two ferries to finish up in the town of El Chaltén, Argentina, where the pavement starts again and you can begin a fresh South American adventure.

VILLA LA ANGOSTURA TO SAN MARTÍN DE LOS ANDES, PATAGONIA, ARGENTINA

RUTA DE LOS SIETE LAGOS

A postcard-pretty ride through Patagonia's famous Lake District, where the views are as enjoyable as the trail

---

DISTANCE: **70 miles (112 km)**   SURFACE: **Paved**   LENGTH OF TRIP: **2 to 3 days**
WHEN TO GO: **November or March (spring or autumn in the Southern Hemisphere)**
DIFFICULTY: **Easy to moderate**

The Ruta de los Siete Lagos (Route of the Seven Lakes) is one of the most famous roads in Argentina, winding 70 miles (112 km) through the heart of the country's gorgeous Lake District in northern Patagonia. Although the route is called the Seven Lakes, it's a rare case of underselling: There are more than seven lakes here. By exploring some of the gravel side tracks that branch off the main paved road, you'll find there are no fewer than 13 lakes to be admired along the way, each of them shimmering in some dazzling shade of blue to which you can't quite pin a name.

The route begins in the picturesque alpine village of Villa la Angostura and heads north to the larger resort town of San Martín de los Andes, meandering from one gorgeous national park to another, through ever changing landscapes of towering snow-clad mountains, meadows of wildflowers, and, of course, these mirrorlike glacial lakes—one of which is actually named Lago Espejo (Mirror Lake).

The Lake District is beautiful any time of year, but because of its popularity, shoulder seasons tend to be the quietest. Autumn offers beautiful foliage, and spring has its wildflowers.

OPPOSITE: Breaks during a tour in the Lake District of Argentina include picturesque views of the area's glacier-fed lakes.

HUASCARÁN CIRCUIT

Pass through the world's loftiest road tunnel at 15,535 feet (4,735 m) on this iconic route through the high Peruvian Andes.

DISTANCE: 143 miles (230 km)   **SURFACE:** Mixed   **LENGTH OF TRIP:** 4 to 6 days
WHEN TO GO: June through September (dry season)   **DIFFICULTY:** Challenging

A legendary ride among expedition cyclists, Peru's Huascarán Circuit offers classic high-altitude Andean adventure. Over 143 breathtaking miles (230 km), the circuit takes you through the spectacular Cordillera Blanca (White Range) mountains on a loop around Peru's highest peak: the towering 22,205-foot (6,768 m) Huascarán. Along the way, you cross two of the most spectacular passes in the Andes and pass through the world's highest road tunnel, at 15,535 feet (4,735 m).

From Lima, catch an eight-hour bus ride to the provincial capital of Carhuaz, 21 miles (34 km) north of Huaraz. Head for the ranger station at the entrance of Huascarán National Park, a 15-mile (24 km) ride that takes you up another 3,000 feet (914 m), no small ask when the town you're leaving is already at an elevation of nearly 9,000 feet (2,745 m). By the time you reach the park entrance, the air is noticeably cooler as you pedal through a landscape of wildflowers and alpine grasses with glacier-clad peaks towering above you. The road continues its inexorable climb—back and forth on some 30 hairpin switchbacks!—as it ascends the flanks of Punta Olímpica to the portal of the world's highest road tunnel at 15,535 feet (4,735 m). From here you can either pedal through the nearly mile-long (1.6 km) tunnel or,

OPPOSITE: Mountain biking in the Cordillera Blanca (White Range) mountains, part of the Andes, in Ancash, Peru

PAGES 154-55: A series of switchbacks lines the mountainside on the Huascarán Circuit.

if you're still feeling your oats at this altitude, continue another two miles (3.2 km) up the rough-and-tumble old road, which claws its way over the top of the pass at 16,204 feet (4,938 m); then brace yourself for the white-knuckle descent on the other side.

Whichever way you choose to do Punta Olímpica, once across you have an exhilarating 19-mile-long (31 km) descent to the town of Chacas, losing 5,000 feet (1,524 m) of elevation along the way. Once again you embark on a climb, this time up and over 13,400-foot (4,084 m) Pupash Pass, pedaling through picturesque villages and alpine wilderness on a quiet gravel road where the only traffic you're likely to encounter are herds of cattle and sheep. The descent on the far side of the pass brings you to Yanama, another of the mountain towns.

You're now on the far side of Huascarán from where you began. It's time to close the loop. From Yanama you begin a 21-mile (34 km) climb back

CYCLING THROUGH HISTORY

What's in a name? The Punta Olímpica, one of the world's most spectacular mountain highways, was named in honor of the Peruvian soccer team that competed in the 1936 Olympics in Berlin, beating Austria 4–2 in a bitterly contested match. Afterward, Austria was granted a rematch because Peruvian fans had invaded the pitch. The entire Peruvian Olympic team withdrew from the games in protest. Back in Peru and high in the Andes, patriotic surveyors who were laying out a route for a new highway named it in honor of the team.

ABOVE: Illuminated campsites perch in the dark on the Cordillera Blanca.

OPPOSITE: An expedition bike on the roadside in Peru

over the shoulders of the Cordillera Blanca on a reasonably good gravel road over the pass at Portachuelo de Llanganuco, at more than 15,400 feet (4,695 m). The payoff for all this hard slogging is some of the most spectacular panoramic views along the whole circuit and the feeling of accomplishment as you crest this high Andean pass on a narrow road carved into the rock. The descent is one long adrenaline rush, swooping through endless switchbacks and on loose gravel, and then back to your starting point at Carhuaz.

This is a loop best done counterclockwise. By starting in Carhuaz and heading for Punta Olímpica first, you can ease yourself into the adventure on paved roads as far as the tunnel and, despite the high altitude, fairly gentle grades. Wild camping is allowed in Huascarán National Park, and towns such as Chacas, Yanama, and Llanganuco along the route have guesthouses if you want to take a break from camping.

SALAR DE UYUNI

Pedal an alien landscape on the planet's largest salt pan.

DISTANCE: **189 miles (304 km)**   SURFACE: **Mixed; salt pan, sand, rock**   LENGTH OF TRIP: **5 to 7 days**
WHEN TO GO: **June through September (dry season)**   DIFFICULTY: **Challenging**

Cycling Salar de Uyuni, Bolivia's remarkable salt flats, is one of the great South American bucket-list rides. The world's largest salt pan, Salar de Uyuni spreads across more than 4,000 square miles (10,360 sq km) on Bolivia's high altiplano. Find yourself surrounded by a vast emptiness of dazzling white salt and taut blue skies where time ceases to have meaning and perspectives and distances become warped.

The classic route starts at Sabaya—accessible by bus from La Paz—giving you not just one staggeringly vast salt pan to ride across but a second one as well. Sabaya is the gateway to the Salar de Coipasa, a smaller—a mere 960 square miles (2,486 sq km)!—but equally haunting salt pan just north of Salar de Uyuni. Together they create an unforgettable weeklong adventure as you pedal south to Uyuni.

This is a challenging ride. While there may be no hills to climb or tricky descents, these dead-flat salt pans are at 12,000 feet (3,657 m), where the air is thin and cold. And there are no windbreaks out here, which is why most cyclists ride north to south, to move with the prevailing northwesterly winds.

The surface of the Coipasa salt pan is softer than that of the rock-hard Salar de Uyuni, and the few miles of rough track linking these two huge salt pans are a tough push of deep sand and rock. Once out on the Salar de Uyuni, the emptiness can be almost overwhelming. Your next goal is Isla Incahuasi, an island of rock, where a quirky, friendly little village gives you a chance to restock supplies before heading out into the desolation once more for the finish line in Uyuni.

KNOW BEFORE YOU GO

Salt is unkind to bicycles; give your bike a thorough cleaning after your crossing. While the summer rains turn the salt pans into the world's largest mirror, making for spectacular photos, the best time for riding is in winter. Dress warmly. It can be bitterly cold at night.

OPPOSITE: The memorable—and blinding—Bolivian salt flats, the world's largest salt pan

LA RUTA DE LOS CONQUISTADORES

Crocodiles, volcanoes, and *Indiana Jones*–style adventure along Costa Rica's muddy jungle tracks on the world's toughest mountain bike race

DISTANCE: 170 miles (275 km)   **SURFACE: Jungle track**   **LENGTH OF TRIP: 3 days**
WHEN TO GO: November   **DIFFICULTY: Extreme**

Since its founding in 1993, the coast-to-coast La Ruta de los Conquistadores (Route of the Conquerors) race through the jungle-clad mountains and volcanoes of Costa Rica has achieved legendary status as the world's toughest mountain bike race. A three-day event staged every year, the course varies slightly each year but approximates the route taken by 17th-century conquistadores, who slashed their way through these steamy jungles in search of gold.

Costa Rica is famed for its lush rainforests and wildlife, and competitors get to experience it all, from dazzlingly bright macaws to colorful poison dart frogs to the possibility of glimpsing a jaguar. The race starts on the Pacific side and crosses a spine of volcanic mountains to reach the Caribbean, passing along the way through muddy jungles, across rivers where crocodiles are a distinct possibility, and up the steep slopes of volcanoes. It's an *Indiana Jones* adventure on two wheels, with more than 20,000 feet (6,095 m) of elevation gain, searing heat, torrential rains, chilly mists on the heights of the volcanoes, and stunningly beautiful rainforests.

Competitors are given 12 hours to finish each of the three daylong stages. Only about half the starters finish the race. For those who fancy

OPPOSITE: Riders carry their bicycles across a railroad bridge on La Ruta de los Conquistadores in Limón, Costa Rica.

PAGES 162-63: A rider zips past lush farmland in Costa Rica.

experiencing this muddy jungle adventure but without the pressure of a timeline and at a less challenging pace, local outfitters offer their knowledge and assistance on multiday trips that take in the same jungle tracks.

If you're in search of an encore challenge beyond the jungles of Costa Rica after tackling La Ruta de los Conquistadores, consider the Absa Cape Epic. The brainchild of South African mountain biker Kevin Vermaak, it's a grueling eight-day mountain bike race through South Africa's Western Cape Province. Vermaak came up with the idea while competing in the 2002 Ruta de los Conquistadores. The route varies but is typically about 450 miles (725 km). The event, a highlight on the pro circuit, is open to amateurs as well. It's said to be the world's most televised mountain bike race and is the only eight-day mountain bike race rated *hors catégorie*—beyond categorization—by the worldwide cyclists governing body, the Union Cycliste Internationale.

Cross both routes off your bucket list and gain a pair of truly epic experiences worth bragging about.

TRANS ECUADOR MTB ROUTE

Towering volcanoes, panama hats, colorful Andean market towns, and Inca ruins in the high Ecuadorian Andes

DISTANCE: **657 miles (1,057 km)**   SURFACE: **Mixed**   LENGTH OF TRIP: **3 weeks**
WHEN TO GO: **June through September (dry season)**   DIFFICULTY: **Challenging to extreme**

I n 1802 when the naturalist Alexander von Humboldt was exploring the Ecuadorian Andes, he found himself traversing a particularly spectacular corridor of mountains he dubbed the Avenue of the Volcanoes—a far more evocative name than the rather bland-sounding Trans Ecuador Mountain Bike Route, which now covers much the same ground. But whatever you wish to call it, this is a stunning ride through the high Andes.

It starts in the picturesque provincial capital of Cuenca, nestled in the mountains. Aside from its beautiful setting and architecture, and easy access by plane or bus from Quito, Cuenca is also famous for panama hats—as many a trivia buff may tell you, panama hats are a uniquely Ecuadorian product, and Cuenca is where the vast majority of them are woven.

From here the route winds its way north between some of South America's highest and most impressive volcanoes: peaks such Cotopaxi, Quilotoa, and Chimborazo—which, at 20,702 feet (6,309 m), was reckoned to be the highest mountain in the world back in Humboldt's day. Along the way, the route passes old Inca ruins and through a chain of colorful Andean market towns.

While it is far from an easy ride—it involves more than 100,000 feet (30,480 m) of climbing and reaches an elevation of 14,780 feet (4,505 m)—this glorious South American adventure is hard to beat.

OPPOSITE: The Trans Ecuador Mountain Bike Route winds through the snowcapped mountains of the high Andes.

PART TWO

EUROPE

Little Langdale in the English Lake District, with the rolling Coniston Fells mountains in the distance

KING ALFRED'S WAY

An off-road cavalcade of history from the prehistoric to the medieval along some of England's most ancient byways

DISTANCE: 218 miles (350 km) **SURFACE:** Mixed; mainly off-road **LENGTH OF TRIP:** 5 to 7 days
WHEN TO GO: Spring through autumn **DIFFICULTY:** Moderate to challenging

Pedal through more than 5,000 years of British history along this mainly off-road bikepacking loop that takes in Stonehenge, Avebury, the Iron Age hill fort at Old Sarum, the sixth-century ruins of Barbury Castle, the medieval cathedrals of Salisbury and Winchester, and miles of rolling green, quintessentially English landscapes.

The circular trail starts and finishes at the landmark bronze statue of King Alfred the Great in Winchester, where the ninth-century Saxon king was originally buried before his remains were removed by monks in 1100 and reinterred at a nearby monastery. Once clear of town, the route sticks to country lanes, bridleways, ancient footpaths, and segments of national hiking trails that have been upgraded for cycling as it meanders through the diverse landscapes of Hampshire, Wiltshire, Berkshire, and Surrey.

Highlights of the ride include the 13th-century Salisbury Cathedral (its spire, at 404 feet/123 meters, is the tallest church spire in England) and the haunting stone circle at Stonehenge on Salisbury Plain. Built in stages on a site that has been in use since Mesolithic times, its iconic ring of sarsen stones dates from 2500 B.C. and is at the heart of a broad historic landscape rich in Neolithic barrows and Bronze Age tombs and that includes the Old Sarum Iron Age hill fort.

OPPOSITE: Winchester Cathedral is a historic monument along King Alfred's Way and one of the largest cathedrals in Europe.

PAGES 170-71: Charming views abound along King Alfred's Way near Old Sarum in Wiltshire.

Even more picturesque are the Neolithic ruins at Avebury. Here the ambitions of Britain's Stone Age monument builders reached their zenith, with an enormous earthwork henge and the biggest stone circle in Europe, more than 1,000 feet (305 m) in diameter—so vast that the village itself lies within it.

History becomes even more vivid as you pedal along the Ridgeway, an ancient bridleway that is reputedly Britain's oldest road, dating back thousands of years. As you close the loop back to Winchester, the final stretch follows along the Pilgrims' Way, a prehistoric track revived by medieval pilgrims traveling from Wessex to the shrine of Thomas à Becket in Canterbury. While the route is surprisingly remote in places, there are also plenty of villages along the way. And the rail connections with towns along the route, such as Salisbury, Swindon, and Reading, mean you can do the trail in stages if you like. It is a route for gravel and mountain bikes rather than tourers.

King Alfred's Way varies in difficulty with the weather. Be very British and check the forecast before you go.

ARMCHAIR RIDE

As a child of Caribbean immigrants growing up in East London, Jools Walker found escapist joy in her hand-me-down BMX bike. Years later, at 28, despite having not sat on a bicycle in ages, she bought herself an elegant Pashley Princess and started commuting to her job in London, rediscovering the joys of getting about on two wheels. Read the tale in her book, *Back in the Frame.*

CICLABILE DELLE DOLOMITI

Cycle the Italian Alps, but without the hills, on Italy's most beautiful rails-to-trails path.

DISTANCE: **37 miles (59 km)**   SURFACE: **Mixed; crushed gravel, paved**
LENGTH OF TRIP: **1 day**   WHEN TO GO: **Spring or early autumn**   DIFFICULTY: **Easy**

Said to be one of Italy's most beautiful rails-to-trails routes, Ciclabile delle Dolomiti (Cycle Path of the Dolomites) offers 37 miles (59 km) of nearly traffic-free pedaling through some of northern Italy's most spectacular mountain scenery.

The route follows the line of an old mountain railway that was originally opened in 1921 to connect the towns of Calalzo di Cadore and Dobbiaco, with the town of Cortina d'Ampezzo, site of the 1956 Winter Olympics, at the midpoint. Starting in Calalzo in the historic Venetian Cadore region and pedaling north, you climb through forests and along the banks of beautiful Alpine lakes, enjoying panoramic views of the peaks towering overhead and crossing the pre-1918 border with Austria along the way. The ride requires a bit more than 1,000 feet (305 m) of elevation gain, but since the path runs along an old railway bed, there are no steep gradients to worry about—a rarity if you're cycling in the Dolomites—leaving you free to enjoy the chocolate-box scenery without all the usual hard work.

OPPOSITE: The jagged edges of the Italian Dolomites frame Ciclabile delle Dolomiti.

DANUBE CYCLE PATH

Waltz along the banks of Europe's grandest river from the medieval town of Passau to the imperial grandeur of Vienna on a delightful purpose-built cycle path.

DISTANCE: 200 miles (322 km)   **SURFACE:** Mainly paved   **LENGTH OF TRIP:** 5 to 7 days
WHEN TO GO: Spring through autumn   **DIFFICULTY:** Easy

If you were to cycle the entire Danube Cycle Path, you'd start in Donaueschingen in Germany's Black Forest and pedal all the way into the heart of Budapest, Hungary, some 750 miles (1,205 km) away. From start to finish it's one of the loveliest long-haul bicycle rides you could ever hope to find, but where it passes through Austria it outdoes itself.

These 200 miles (322 km), from the postcard-pretty river town of Passau on the German-Austria border to the imperial grandeur of Vienna, are like some glorious old continental travel poster brought to life—an endlessly scrolling cavalcade of picturesque villages and onion-domed churches near riverbanks, vineyards, orchards, and dark European forests with brooding castles, as this river shimmers beside you the whole way. It is an easy jaunt—an achievable adventure—and because of that you'll find whole families riding this segment of the trail, and because of them you'll find the towns and villages along the way are wonderfully bicycle-friendly.

The ride starts in Passau, where the Inn and the Ilz Rivers join the Danube, and follows the now bigger, statelier Danube downstream toward Vienna, running along old towpaths from the days when horses pulled barges along the river, dedicated bicycle trails, and quiet country lanes. The gradients

PHOTO OP

Take a break at the village of Schlögen, about 25 miles (40 km) from the start at Passau, and hike up the trail to a scenic lookout over the river. It's about a 30-minute walk and steep, but the view to the northwest of the 180-degree bend in the Danube, known as the Schlögener Schlinge, is sensational.

OPPOSITE: Catch a ferry across the Danube River.

PAGES 176-77: The stunning view of the vineyard-covered hills of Wachau as seen from the ruins of Hinterhaus Castle in the historic village of Spitz

are gentle, where there are any at all, and the scenery rustic. Indeed, the only city you'll pass through the whole way across Austria is Linz, about halfway to Vienna, and even there you can keep to the wooded banks on the opposite side of the river if you prefer. For much of its length, the Danube Cycle Path runs along both banks, with bicycle ferries making it easy and fun to hop across the river, either to ride through shady sections of forest on sultry afternoons or pass through villages where you can see the sights, replenish supplies, or indulge in a "radler"—the cyclist's tipple, a refreshing mix of beer and lemonade—in one of the pubs.

Highlights include the iconic bend in the river at Schlögen, where you can climb—on foot—up a steep wooded ridge for a magnificent view over the Danube; the exquisitely beautiful Wachau Valley, with its terraced orchards and vineyards that date back to the time of Charlemagne; the ruined castle at Dürnstein, where Richard the Lionheart was

CYCLING THROUGH HISTORY

The terraced vineyards in the Wachau Valley date back more than 1,000 years. Riesling and Grüner Veltliner are the main grape varieties here. All the wines in the valley are made using only locally grown grapes according to the Codex Wachau, a strict set of rules designed to preserve the area's ancient traditions.

ABOVE: The bike path
follows the banks of
the Danube River into
a colorful village in the
Wachau Valley.

OPPOSITE: Break time
near Befreiungshalle (Hall
of Liberation) with a view
of the Danube Valley

imprisoned on his way back to England; and the overblown opulence of the Benedictine monastery at Melk, whose onion-domed towers dominate the landscape for miles.

The final 50 miles (80 km) of the ride are flat and fast along the river floodplain as it approaches Vienna, the grand finale. Even here the path retains its rural flavor until the last minute, approaching the imperial city through the foothills of the fabled Vienna woods, then guiding you into the center along a series of excellent traffic-free bike paths. Finish off this cycling idyll in style by calling in at one of Vienna's grand old fin de siècle cafés for a Turkish coffee and slice of apple strudel. Café Landtmann on the Ringstrasse is a classic.

DANISH NORTH COAST BICYCLE ROUTE 47

Here's where bicycle-happy Danes ride for a perfect weekend getaway.

DISTANCE: **40 miles (64 km)**   SURFACE: **Mixed; dedicated bicycle path**   LENGTH OF TRIP: **I day**
WHEN TO GO: **Anytime**   DIFFICULTY: **Easy**

Bicycle-friendly Denmark has more delightful cycle routes than you can shake a stick at, but one that seems to make everyone's short list of favorites is the North Coast Bicycle Route 47.

With both end points easily accessible by train from Copenhagen, this smooth, flat ride along the so-called Danish Riviera offers a cavalcade of white-sand swimming beaches, seascapes, pine forests, fishing villages, seaside towns, ice-cream parlors, and endless views over the Kattegat, the lake-like sea that separates Denmark's Jutland Peninsula from Sweden. The ride can be done in a couple of hours on a road bike, if you've a mind to go fast; it can also be a leisurely getaway spread out over several days, with plenty of attractive hotels and B&Bs along the way.

Aside from the classic seaside attractions of surf, sand, and ice cream, there's a museum of modern art at Nivå, along with a bird reserve and rhododendron gardens at Nivaagaard. There's a water mill (now a café) in the forest, a picturesque lighthouse, a museum and sculpture garden dedicated to the works of the early 20th-century sculptor Rudolph Tegner, and lovely views of Kronborg Castle, the castle in which Shakespeare set *Hamlet*.

OPPOSITE: **Visit the Nakke-hoved Lighthouse and the Lighthouse History Museum near the Kattegat strait on the north coast of Denmark.**

PARIS-BREST-PARIS

Write yourself into history and become one of the *anciens* of the world's oldest and most prestigious cycling event, dating back to 1891.

DISTANCE: **763 miles (1,228 km)**   SURFACE: **Paved**   LENGTH OF TRIP: **90 hours—or less!**
WHEN TO GO: **August, every four years**   DIFFICULTY: **Extreme**

The legendary Paris-Brest-Paris ride is said to be the world's oldest ongoing cycling event, started in 1891, only a bare few years after the newfangled modern bicycle took to the streets and consigned the penny-farthing to history. Bicycles and bicycle racing were all the rage at the time, and with a canny eye on readership and advertising, the editor of French newspaper *Le Petit Journal* announced that a heroic new race would be held that summer from Paris to Brest and back again, 763 miles (1,228 km) nonstop—first across the line wins.

More than 400 cyclists signed up for the event, with 100 actually finishing, the winner in 72 hours—a time that would be very creditable on a modern bike today. Thousands turned up in the streets of Paris to watch the finish. And with that, a tradition was born. Jump forward more than 130 years, and Paris-Brest-Paris—or PBP, as it's referred to in cycling literature—has evolved into the world's most prestigious cycling event, steeped in history and attracting more than 6,000 entrants from around the globe, all hoping to complete the ride within the 90-hour time limit.

Although it started out as a professional race, Paris-Brest-Paris has been open to all for the better part of a century. These days, that means anyone who completes a series of qualifying long-distance rides at sanctioned

OPPOSITE: **A grassy spot to stretch out on the Paris-Brest-Paris route**

PAGES 184-85: **Riders are welcomed into Mortagne-au-Perche during Paris-Brest-Paris.**

events in the months leading up to the race. And while it was originally held every 10 years, it has taken place every four since 1975.

Riders must be completely self-supporting—no support vehicles or helpers allowed—carrying everything they need in terms of clothing, tools, and spares, and buying food and drink along the way. It is essentially a form of fast, light touring—a sport known as randonneuring—and more like a rally than a race, with the emphasis on completion rather than winning, although the top riders move along at a considerable pace and ride around the clock. The record for completing Paris-Brest-Paris is under 44 hours.

While the event is called Paris-Brest-Paris, the ride actually starts in the town of Rambouillet, about 12 miles (19 km) south of the city. The route traditionally followed the main road from Paris to Brittany, but with the growth of highway traffic over the years, the route has shifted onto smaller,

BREAKOUT

You needn't be a cyclist to enjoy a Paris-Brest. It is also the name of a rich French pastry, shaped like a bicycle wheel and created in 1910 by a Parisian pâtissier named Louis Durand in honor of the legendary race. It consists of choux pastry with a praline-buttercream filling and is topped with slivered almonds and a dusting of sugar. Family-owned Pâtisserie Durand is still in business in Paris today. The original Paris-Brest recipe is a closely guarded secret, although that hasn't stopped the world's pastry chefs from turning out their own versions of the delicious treat.

quieter roads. It's a surprisingly hilly ride, involving more than 35,000 feet (10,670 m) of climbing in all, although the impression you get as you pedal along the long, straight stretches is of endlessly rolling countryside rather than big climbs. And as you head into Brittany, wind can become a factor.

Riders are obliged to pass through a series of checkpoints along the way out to Brest, get their cards stamped at each stop, and then tick off that same series of checkpoints in reverse order on the return leg. A festival atmosphere descends on the roads and villages along the route, with thousands of cyclists sharing the experience of riding through the night, the old stone Bretagne villages decorated for the event, and villagers turning out at all hours to cheer on the riders. Every finisher is a winner and can forever after enjoy the lifelong cachet of being one of the *anciens* of Paris-Brest-Paris.

ABOVE: **A rider checks the route stages before dawn.**

OPPOSITE: **Charming French villages dot the Paris-Brest-Paris.**

LAKE CONSTANCE CYCLE PATH

A classic, old-fashioned cycling idyll around one of Europe's most beautiful bodies of water

DISTANCE: 168 miles (270 km)   **SURFACE:** Mostly paved   **LENGTH OF TRIP:** 3 to 5 days
WHEN TO GO: Spring through autumn   **DIFFICULTY:** Easy

Tucked in the northern foothills of the Alps, Lake Constance (Bodensee in German) is widely regarded as one of the most beautiful bodies of water in Europe. Unlike the larger Lake Geneva, which is ringed by highways, Lake Constance is more rural, and the cycle route that loops around it is one of the continent's most popular cycling idylls.

Being a circular route, the Lake Constance Cycle Path can be started anywhere, although the small German lakeside city of Friedrichshafen is a popular beginning. The scenic lakeside city was the home of Ferdinand von Zeppelin, inventor of the dirigible, and was home to the factory that made these grand airships. Today the Zeppelin Museum, located in the old harborside railway station, houses the world's largest collection of airship artifacts and memorabilia, including a 108-foot-long (33 m) walk-in reconstruction of the interior of the *Hindenburg*.

Leaving Friedrichshafen and following the route in a clockwise direction, the path meanders along the shore through farmlands, orchards, and vineyards to Lindau and an area known as the Bavarian Riviera. Lindau's medieval old town is on an island accessible by a pedestrian causeway.

Farther east, the path crosses into Austria, enters Switzerland, and continues along the southern shore of the lake—or rather, lakes. Lake Constance is actually

OPPOSITE: The picturesque view of Lake Constance through the trees

PAGES 190-91: The tree-lined cycle track to Reichenau Island makes for a perfect photo op.

three interconnected bodies of water: the Überlinger See, the Untersee, and the vast Obersee. Konstanz, Germany, is where the three connect.

Konstanz (pop. 85,000), the largest city on the lake, is a vibrant medieval university community. Two nearby islands, both accessible by causeway, are popular draws: Mainau Island, famed for its colorful gardens, and the World Heritage–listed Reichenau Island, whose eighth-century Benedictine abbey was famed for its illuminated manuscripts and frescoes.

From Konstanz, pop back into Switzerland around the fingerlike Überlinger See and Untersee as you close the loop back to the start at Friedrichshafen.

Among the many benefits of cycling the Lake Constance path is that a network of ferries crisscrosses the lake, not only cutting off distance but also allowing you to experience the lake itself. Go in spring to catch the fruit trees in bloom, or go in early autumn, after the summer rush is over but before the winter fog sets in.

REST STOP

View Lake Constance and its castles from a novel perspective and touch base with local history. At Friedrichshafen, the original home of the Graf Zeppelin factory, you can book a flight on a modern zeppelin—weather permitting—and spend a couple of hours cruising at 1,000 feet (305 m) and a stately 45 miles an hour (72 km/h). Twelve different routes around the lake are offered. The capsule on the zeppelins can seat up to 14 passengers, and each seat is a window seat.

LA VÉLODYSSÉE

Explore the wild and beautiful French coast from windswept Brittany down to the border of sunny Spain on France's longest signposted cycleway.

DISTANCE: **750 miles (1,207 km)**   SURFACE: **Varied**   LENGTH OF TRIP: **2 to 3 weeks**
WHEN TO GO: **Spring to early autumn; avoid high season (mid-July to mid-August)**
DIFFICULTY: **Easy to moderate**

Start this dream of a ride in the picturesque old spa town of Roscoff. More than 70 percent of the ride's length is traffic free, and the rest unfolds along quiet country lanes. Begin by pedaling inland from Roscoff along greenways and cycle paths to join the towpath of the famed Nantes-Brest Canal and follow it south to Nantes. The historic canal, the longest in France at some 240 miles (385 km), with 238 locks, opened to great fanfare in 1842, and for decades was the conduit by which Brittany's market gardeners shipped their produce to cities down south. Today the old canal's cinder towpath is one of the country's most scenic cycleways.

At Nantes the Vélodyssée rejoins the coast, meandering through forests, salt marshes, and sand dunes, market towns and glamorous old seaside resorts, on its way down to the town of Hendaye on the border of Spain. Highlights along the way are the 15th-century fortress town of La Rochelle; the fishing town of Marennes, famed for its oysters; and the belle epoque resorts of Arcachon and Biarritz. Given the easy accessibility by rail to towns along the Vélodyssée, it is possible to do it in bite-size stages if you don't have time to do the entire route. For those looking for adventure on a still grander scale, the 750-mile (1,207 km) Vélodyssée is itself merely the French section of EuroVelo 1, a 6,835-mile (11,000 km) route stretching from the far north of Norway to Portugal's Algarve.

OPPOSITE: The medieval Josselin Castle on the banks of the canal from Nantes to Brest dates to the early 11th century.

LÔN LAS CYMRU

Discover the breathtaking landscapes that inspired 18th-century painters in this lyrical ride through Wales.

DISTANCE: 237 miles (381 km)   **SURFACE: Mixed**   **LENGTH OF TRIP: 3 to 6 days**
WHEN TO GO: Spring through autumn   **DIFFICULTY: Moderate to challenging**

One of the most beautiful cycling routes in Britain, Lôn Las Cymru literally takes you through the countryside for which the word "picturesque" was coined by the Romantic artists of the late 18th century—notably William Gilpin in his 1782 treatise *Observations on the River Wye, and Several Parts of South Wales*. Starting in the medieval castle town of Chepstow on the banks of the River Severn (an alternate start in Cardiff is available), you amble on quiet country lanes through the very countryside Gilpin praised, into the Black Mountains and up the idyllic Vale of Ewyas. Pass the "picturesque" ruins of the 12th-century Llanthony Priory, whose melancholy beauty drew painters such as J. M. W. Turner, and climb up to the crest of Gospel Pass, the highest pass in Wales, at 1,778 feet (542 m), and arguably the most beautiful pass in Britain. The view over the Wye Valley from the top is worth every stroke of the pedals you make to get there.

Then take a long, breezy serpentine descent to Hay-on-Wye, a book lover's paradise whose streets are lined with wonderfully musty secondhand and antique bookshops and whose annual literary festival draws writers from all over the world.

Over the next few days the route takes you through the ancient Cambrian Mountains, across the Desert of Wales—yes, there is such a thing: an astonishingly desolate stretch of moorlands in the center of the country—and skirts the mountainous wilds of Snowdonia. Welsh mountains may not

OPPOSITE: **The rolling hills of Gospel Pass in Brecon Beacons make for a scenic trek through Wales.**

PAGES 196-97: **A cyclist ascends a hill near the town of Porthmadog on the Lôn Las Cymru.**

be particularly high, but they are rugged and spectacular; there's a reason the British Army's Special Air Service do their survival training in Wales.

The Lôn Las Cymru isn't all mountains and granny-gearing up steep country lanes. There are some delightfully easy stretches of rails-to-trails to be enjoyed as well, such as the nine miles (14.4 km) where the route follows the Mawddach Trail, widely regarded as one of Britain's prettiest rails-to-trails routes. It picks it up at the handsome gray-stone market town of Dolgellau and runs along the hauntingly beautiful Mawddach Estuary to the old seaside town of Barmouth, where it crosses the mouth of the estuary on a grand old wooden railway bridge.

A little farther north, the 12.5-mile (20.1 km) run along the Lôn Eifion Cycleway offers a smooth, leafy ride from Bryncir in northwestern Wales into the medieval fortress town Caernarfon, with its imposing walls surrounding the town and massive 13th-century castle, one of four huge World

BREAKOUT

Shortly after you cross the Menai Bridge onto Anglesey, you'll see road signs for the town of Llanfair P.G. It's worth taking a detour here for a photo op at the train station, where the elongated sign spells out the town's glorious name in full: Llanfairpwllgwyngyllgogery-chwyrndrobwllllantysiliogogogoch. At 58 letters and 18 syllables, it's the longest place-name in Europe and the second longest in the world. (Incredibly, New Zealand's Maori people have an even longer one, at 85 letters!)

Heritage-listed castles built by Edward I to guard his remote northwestern Welsh frontier.

From Caernarfon the trail hugs the Menai Strait for a few miles before crossing over onto the Isle of Anglesey on the historic Menai Bridge, built by the engineer Thomas Telford in 1826 and regarded as the world's first major suspension bridge. This is the final leg of the trail, a gentle ride along the coast to the ferry port of Holyhead, the jumping-off point for ferries to Ireland. Indeed, the official end of the trail is the parking lot at the ferry terminal, but rather than have such a tame end to your ride, it's far better to press on another couple of miles and finish up at the haunting South Stack Lighthouse.

ABOVE: The distinctive track marker in Porthma-dog, Gwynedd, Wales

OPPOSITE: The multistory Richard Booth's Bookshop in Hay-on-Wye, Wales

L'EROICA

One for the cycling romantics: an astonishingly beautiful ride through Tuscany's sun-bronzed landscapes on its famous white gravel roads

DISTANCE: **130 miles (209 km)**　SURFACE: **Mixed**　LENGTH OF TRIP: **1 to 3 days**
WHEN TO GO: **Spring and autumn**　DIFFICULTY: **Challenging**

A celebration of the heroic age of cycling on rural Italy's picturesque strade bianche (white gravel roads), L'Eroica is an annual event for vintage bicycles held each October in Tuscany and Siena. Entrants ride bicycles built before 1987—no clipless pedals allowed—and dress at least in "classically inspired" cycling gear, if not necessarily vintage clothing. Many dress up like old-time Giro d'Italia riders and pedal century-old racers—the event can often look wonderfully like an old sepia print come to life.

Since its inception in 1997, L'Eroica has become a sought-after bucket-list ride for cycling romantics the world over. Because of this popularity, registration numbers are limited. For those who can't make it to Italy in October, can't get an entry, or don't own vintage bicycles, organizers have created a permanent signposted course so that it is possible to ride L'Eroica anytime on any sort of bicycle—even an electric one—and take in the region's glorious landscapes and equally glorious wines, olives, honeys, and cheeses.

The route starts in Gaiole in the Chianti region and makes a grand loop through the hot, yellow landscapes of Siena and Tuscany, along roads lined with cypresses and vineyards, past villas, and through medieval villages. It is a challenging ride involving nearly 12,000 feet (3,660 m) of elevation gain. One of the most strenuous stretches, and yet most scenic, is the climb up Castiglion del Bosco to Montalcino. The view over the achingly beautiful Val d'Orcia highlights rolling vineyards and sun-bronzed fields of wheat. From there, close the loop, taking in the legendary climb up Monte Sante Marie to bring you back to Gaiole.

OPPOSITE: **A cyclist on a vintage bicycle trains for L'Eroica near Gaiole in Chianti, Italy.**

MONT VENTOUX

Ride through lavender fields and along the stunning Gorges de la Nesque to the iconic summit of the Giant of Provence.

DISTANCE: **52 miles (84 km)**   SURFACE: **Paved**   LENGTH OF TRIP: **I day**
WHEN TO GO: **Mid-June through mid-July**   DIFFICULTY: **Challenging**

Mont Ventoux is one of the most storied climbs in the history of the Tour de France—and the scene of one of the tour's greatest tragedies, when in 1967 the indomitable British cycling star Tom Simpson literally rode himself to death while racing up the mountain's flanks on a scorching July day during the ill-fated stage 13 of the race. Simpson famously asked in his dying breath to be put back on his bicycle. Simpson's Byronic death less than a mile from the summit, coupled with the mountain's long history in the Tour de France and the sheer physical challenge of pedaling up it, has made conquering Mont Ventoux a bucket-list ride for bicycle-racing romantics the world over.

Three routes lead to the summit of Ventoux, one from the north and two from the south. The toughest of the three is the classic approach from the village of Bedoin, the route favored by the Tour de France. The ride suggested here is a longer and more scenic variation on the classic route up Ventoux, combining a ride through the beautiful Gorges de la Nesque with the legendary climb for one of the most spectacular and challenging road bike circuits in France.

Start in the old market town of Sault, in the heart of Provence's lavender country, and pedal south along the D942 into the Gorges de la Nesque. For 13 miles (21 km), between Monieux and Villes-sur-Auzon, you wind your way along the cliff face of the gorge on one of the most dramatic "balcony roads" in France, with stunning views of the gorge—more than 1,000 feet (305 m)

OPPOSITE: The famous lavender fields of Provence splash color and charm along the route.

PAGES 204-5: A cyclist climbs Mont Ventoux, with the summit in sight in the background.

deep in places—and glimpses of Mont Ventoux, hazy in the distance.

As beautiful as this route is, the Tour de France has never passed through here. The narrowness of the road, with its hairpin curves and one-lane tunnels, can't accommodate the race's caravans and support vehicles, qualities that make this lovely road all the more appealing for independent cyclists, as few regular motorists use it either. It's also beautifully quiet.

The ascent up Mont Ventoux starts shortly after the gorge near the village of Sainte-Colombe, where you join the classic route to the summit. After a long, steep climb through the forest, you emerge above the tree line at Chalet Reynaud into the famously bleak lunar landscape of Mont Ventoux's upper flanks. From here it is just under four miles (6.4 km) to the summit. While the climbing is not as steep as it was farther down the mountain, these last few miles are the toughest. There's no

CYCLING THROUGH HISTORY

During the 2016 edition of the Tour de France, race leader Chris Froome found himself caught up in a crash with a motorcycle half a mile (0.8 km) from the day's finish line. With his bike broken, the indomitable Englishman famously set off on foot, running for the Mont Ventoux summit, until a fresh bike could be had. Mont Ventoux is arguably where the idea of tourism and the sport of mountain climbing got its start, when the Italian poet Francesco Petrarch hiked to the summit in 1336 purely out of curiosity. His 6,000-word essay "The Ascent of Mont Ventoux" invited a new way of looking at nature.

ABOVE: Conquer the world-famous climb and reach the marker for the summit and spectacular views.

OPPOSITE: A breathtaking view during the ascent

shade anywhere, nor any shelter from the powerful mistral winds if they happen to be blowing. And if they aren't blowing, the heat radiating from the rock can easily raise the temperature another 10 or even 20 degrees Fahrenheit (5.5 to 11°C).

Half a mile (0.8 km) or so below the summit, you pass the memorial to Tom Simpson, erected near where he fell that day. For many riders, for whom Mont Ventoux is a pilgrimage, this is a place to pause and pay respects before pressing on to the summit. The descent is down the same road on which you came up, but this time taking the left-hand fork when you reach Chalet Reynaud and continuing downhill to your starting point back in Sault.

THE RING ROAD

Haunting desolation and otherworldly beauty on a lonely highway around Iceland

DISTANCE: **820 miles (1,320 km)**   SURFACE: **Mostly paved**   LENGTH OF TRIP: **2 weeks**
WHEN TO GO: **June through August**   DIFFICULTY: **Challenging**

Iceland has some of the most dramatic landscapes on Earth, and there's no better way to see and experience them than from the saddle of a bicycle on this hauntingly desolate highway—aka Route 1—that circumnavigates the island. Given the remoteness and the blustery North Atlantic weather, a cycling tour around Iceland is nothing to be taken lightly, but if you are fit and well prepared, this is one of the world's great accessible adventures.

Iceland's pretty little capital, Reykjavík, is the starting point, with most riders choosing to ride the loop in a counterclockwise direction, pedaling first along the south coast. It is flatter here, and not quite as remote as later sections of the ride. By doing this section first, you ease yourself into the rhythms of the land and find your expedition legs before tackling the altogether hillier and more isolated northern sections.

But even in the south, the sense of outback adventure gets under way pretty quickly. More than 70 percent of Icelanders live in or around their capital city, and once you're clear of Reykjavík, the road and the scenery open up around you as you pedal into a magical world of glaciers, volcanoes, waterfalls, marshes, black sand deserts, and towering cliffs. It is virtually impossible to get lost along the route; just follow this one lonely ribbon of highway, which occasionally narrows to an even more ribbonlike single lane on some of the bridges.

Among the many highlights along the southern coast are the great waterfalls at Seljalandsfoss and Skògafoss, the famous black sand beaches near Vík,

OPPOSITE: **A lone cyclist takes on the Ring Road near Skaftafell, part of Vatnajökull National Park, in southeast Iceland.**

PAGES 210-11: **Pause on Snaefellsnes Peninsula to take in the mighty Kirkjufell (Church Mountain) and Kirkjufellsfoss (Church Mountain Falls).**

and the beautiful and World Heritage–listed Vatnajökull National Park and Skaftafell nature reserve.

From there the highway meanders through the remote Eastfjords and the Jökulsárlón glacier lagoon, then veers up into the wilder north with the beautiful Lake Mývatn and Akureyri (pop. 19,000)—Iceland's second biggest town, just south of the Arctic Circle. For most of its length, the Ring Road hugs the coast. But as it descends the western flank of the island, it cuts off Snaefellsnes Peninsula and Westfjords—both of which are worthwhile detours if you have the time—before delivering you back to Reykjavík.

Virtually all the Ring Road is open to cyclists, with two exceptions: the three-mile-long (4.8 km) Hvalfjörður Tunnel and around Reykjavík itself. In both cases bicycle-friendly work-arounds are available, with the route around the Hvalfjörður Fjord being a far prettier option to the viewless tunnel. Summer is definitely the best time to go, when the weather is likely to be nicer, and you have the benefit of nearly round-the-clock daylight.

REST STOP

Cyclists the world over often jokingly cite the "Puncture Fairy" as the cause of those inexplicable flat tires that occur every now and then. But in Iceland you may be dealing with the real thing. The existence of Huldufólk, or elves, is taken seriously here. Enroll in the Elf School in Reykjavík for a three-hour course taught by some of Iceland's leading elf and folklore experts. Hafnarfjörður, Borgarfjörður Eystri, Ásbyrgi Canyon, and Bjartmarssteinn are also elven hot spots around the country.

DUNWICH DYNAMO ROUTE

Join the fun on an all-night moonlit ride from the heart of London to the lonely Suffolk coast in this informal British cycling classic.

DISTANCE: **112 miles (180 km)**   SURFACE: **Paved**   LENGTH OF TRIP: **1 night**
WHEN TO GO: **July, on a Saturday nearest the full moon**   DIFFICULTY: **Challenging**

An iconic fixture in the London cycling calendar for more than 30 years, the Dunwich Dynamo is an overnight ride from the city to Dunwich, a tiny village set along a lonely stretch of the Suffolk coast.

A highly social event, the Dunwich Dynamo starts at dusk outside the Pub on the Park in the inner-city neighborhood of Hackney on the Saturday night nearest the full moon. As many as 3,000 cyclists have been known to turn up for the informal event, riding anything from road bikes to tourers, penny-farthings to recumbents, pedaling through the short summer night to witness the sunrise on the beach the following morning. Pop-up food stands along the way sell snacks and drinks to riders as they pass through a string of otherwise sleeping villages along the route.

Summer nights are short in England, and under clear skies the full moon offers a surprising amount of light. Even so, you'll need a good headlamp for the ride, and you'll want to pack plenty of snacks and water as well, in case the food stalls en route are sold out. Sunrise on the beach, after the long night ride from London, is magic. Plan ahead and arrange to have someone pick you up from Dunwich. Few trains serve this stretch of coast, and those that do are quickly overwhelmed. Otherwise, it's a long ride back to the city.

ARMCHAIR RIDE

Emily Chappell found herself intrigued by the picaresque lives of the bicycle couriers who came in and out of her London office in all winds and weathers. And so she quit her job and joined them. The result is *What Goes Around*, an engaging account of life as a bicycle courier in a restless, fast-paced city.

OPPOSITE: Speeding through Finchingfield during the annual Dunwich Dynamo

RHINE CYCLE ROUTE

Follow one of Europe's most beautiful rivers from its source in the Swiss Alps to its mouth at the Hook of Holland.

DISTANCE: **932 miles (1,500 km)**   SURFACE: **Varied**   LENGTH OF TRIP: **2 to 3 weeks**
WHEN TO GO: **Spring through autumn**   DIFFICULTY: **Easy**

The Rhine is one of Europe's grandest rivers, and this course tracks alongside it all the way to where it empties into the North Sea. This almost cinematic bicycle path takes in half a dozen countries and scrolls through a succession of classic continental travel poster–like scenes: Swiss Alps, Rhineland vineyards, Dutch windmills, and countless cathedral cities and fairy-tale castles.

A compilation of quiet country roads, bicycle paths, and gravel tracks that run along the river's banks and levees, the Rhine Cycle Route—also known as EuroVelo 15—is one of Europe's most popular long-haul bike routes and a perfect choice for beginners making their first international cycling expedition.

The ride starts in the Swiss mountain village of Andermatt. Although the Rhine Cycle Route is famously easy to pedal throughout most of its length, the first few miles of it, as you get up into the Alpine heights where the trickling young Rhine has its source, involve some serious climbing: more than 2,000 feet (610 m) of elevation gain on a narrow switchback road to the crest of Oberalp Pass. It's certainly scenic enough, but if you'd rather skip the climb, take the narrow-gauge Matterhorn Gotthard Railway up to Oberalp Pass

OPPOSITE: The steeple of St. Peter's Church rises in the distance in the historic town of Kempen, Germany.

PAGES 216-17: A curving bridge seems to float over the Rhine-Herne Canal near Gelsenkirchen, Germany.

station—elevation 6,719 feet (2,048 m)—and start your journey to the sea there.

The first part of the route, through the upper Rhine Valley to Lake Constance, is something of a roller-coaster ride, with a few steep climbs, some exhilarating descents, and a spectacular run through Ruinaulta, known as Switzerland's Grand Canyon, on a gorgeous "balcony road" that hugs the cliff face. About 80 miles (129 km) into your ride, you have the opportunity to bag a new country on your list: Vaduz, the capital of tiny Liechtenstein, lies just across the river, and there are several bridges to take you across.

Otherwise, Austria is your next border, as you pass through Bregenz on your approach to Lake Constance—or Bodensee as the vast lake is called in German. The Rhine flows into the eastern end of the lake and out again on the western end, so between the Lake Constance Cycle Path (page 188), which circles the lake, and the ferries that cross over it, your options for this next segment of the route are almost unlimited.

PHOTO OP

One of the most beautiful stretches of the Rhine is the 42-mile (68 km) one between Bingen and Koblenz. Known as the Rhine Gorge, it is famed for dozens of medieval castles, terraced vineyards, and the legendary Loreley Rock, a 433-foot-high (132 m) rise on the right bank of the river where, like the Sirens in the *Odyssey,* the bewitchingly beautiful Loreley sat combing her golden hair, distracting boatmen with her beauty and song and luring them to their deaths.

ABOVE: **The charming half-timbered houses of Alsace, France**

OPPOSITE: **There are 19 photo op–worthy UNESCO World Heritage–listed windmills near Dordrecht, Netherlands, built in the mid-18th century.**

On your way out of Schaffhausen, having left the lake behind, you come to the spectacular Rhine Falls, one of the biggest and most powerful waterfalls in Europe. Downstream from here, the river flows through Basel, Switzerland, before veering north to the border between France and Germany. For the next few days, you meander through beautiful riparian forests; the wine country of Alsace, France; pretty medieval villages; the grand old cathedral cities of Strasbourg and Cologne, France; and the industrial heartland of Arnhem, Netherlands—an interesting contrast to the rustic landscapes through which you've been riding. Then comes the vast port city of Rotterdam, the beautiful wetlands and iconic collection of windmills at Kinderdijk, and the sea dunes and the Hook of Holland, where the Rhine empties into the sea.

COSTA BRAVA LOOP

Explore Spanish villages and a medieval fort on this stunning ride along the Catalan coast.

DISTANCE: 56 miles (90 km)   **SURFACE:** Paved   **LENGTH OF TRIP:** 1 day
WHEN TO GO: Spring; early morning is best   **DIFFICULTY:** Moderate

This is a spectacular roller coaster of a ride along Spain's Costa Brava, offering quiet coves, craggy red cliffs, a medieval village, and glorious vistas overlooking the Mediterranean. The route begins in Girona and heads south along quiet backroads some 15 miles (24 km) to Llagostera, where you start the climb into the craggy coastal mountains before a fast descent to the coast leads you to the ancient town of Tossa de Mar.

Known more for vineyards and cork production than fishing (despite its charming seaside location), Tossa de Mar is the only remaining medieval fortified town along the Catalan coast. Pause your trip to visit the old town center or one of the local cafés for a great place to take a break and have lunch ahead of the gorgeous homeward ride.

From Tossa de Mar, follow the beautiful coastal road for six miles (9.6 km) or so east to the turnoff to Sant Grau and the long, winding climb up toward the neo-Romanesque Sant Grau monastery, which sits 1,181 feet (360 m) above the sea. Be sure to pause here for a bit—the views are stupendous and the courtyard is a great place to stop for a drink. Depart from the monastery for a pleasant descent back to Llagostera and a leisurely return to Girona the way you came.

OPPOSITE: Dawn illuminates the historic village of Cadaqués in Catalonia, Spain.

TOUR DE MONT AIGOUAL

Tackle the mountains of the remote Cévennes on the route of cycling's most famous fictional race.

DISTANCE: **85 miles (137 km)**   SURFACE: **Paved**   LENGTH OF TRIP: **1 day**
WHEN TO GO: **Summer, in early morning**   DIFFICULTY: **Challenging**

I n the words of its best known yet famously anonymous participant, the Rider, the Tour de Mont Aigoual is "the sweetest, toughest ride of the season": 85 miles (137 km) of hard, uncompromising racing through a remote, mountainous pocket of the Cévennes. The story of the race as it unfolds on a sultry June day in 1977 forms the narrative of Tim Krabbé's cult classic *The Rider*. Written in the first person—Krabbé himself was a successful amateur racer—*The Rider* is widely acknowledged to be one of the finest portrayals ever written of the intimate thoughts, motivations, and psyche of a racing cyclist during a race.

Vivid though it may be, the book itself is a work of fiction—in real life there is no race called the Tour de Mont Aigoual. But Mont Aigoual and the roads and cols and tricky descents on which this fictional race takes place are all very real indeed. Riding the Tour de Mont Aigoual has become something of a pilgrimage for literary-minded road cyclists since the book first appeared in 1978 (it was translated from Dutch to English in 2002).

The ride starts in Meyrueis, a picturesque town tucked away in the heavily

OPPOSITE: **Cyclists follow the route of the fictional race in *The Rider* by Tim Krabbé as they head into town to cross La Jonte River in southern France.**

PAGES 224-25: **The deep valleys and high peaks of the Causses and the Cévennes are listed as UNESCO World Heritage sites.**

wooded Massif Central in south-central France. The route forms a figure-eight loop through the mountains and involves nearly 9,000 feet (2,745 m) of elevation gain. It gets off to a deceptively easy start with 12 miles (19 km) or so of swift, twisting descent along the beautiful Gorges de la Jonte to the village of Le Rozier. Here, the road crosses the river and continues along the grander and even more spectacular Gorges du Tarn toward the first climb, which has occupied the thoughts of the eponymous Rider in the novel since the peloton left town.

The ascent begins immediately after the village of Les Vignes: three miles (4.8 km) of steep switchbacks climbing out of the gorge to the Causse Méjean, a barren highland plateau whose winds and false flats dampen the spirits of the cyclists in the race after the tough climb. Following a long pull across the plateau, you begin a rapid, harrowing descent back down the gorge to Meyrueis to close the first and smaller loop of the figure-eight course.

ARMCHAIR RIDE

A cult classic among racing cyclists, *The Rider* by Tim Krabbé tells of the thoughts, machinations, and internal philosophizing of an amateur racer as he competes in the fictional Tour de Mont Aigoual, an 85-mile (137 km) race through the mountains in the French Cévennes. It is widely regarded as the best novel about bicycle racing ever written.

Plate-forme
de
L'Observatoire
DU
MONT AIGOUAL

Altitude : 1571ᵐ
Longitude Est : 1° 14′ 40″
Latitude Nord : 44° 7′ 20″

The second loop is where you tackle Mont Aigoual itself. It begins with another steep climb, four miles (6.4 km) this time, upward through the forest to another desolate high plateau, the Causse Noir, where more winds and miles of false flats await before you begin an even more harrowing descent to the village of Trèves, one in which the Rider—a nervous descender—imagines the consequences of missing a curve and flying off into the abyss.

Trèves marks the start of the ultimate climb, a relentless 16 miles (26 km) to the high point of the race, just beneath the summit of Mont Aigoual, which, at 5,141 feet (1,567 m), is among the highest mountains in the Cévennes. A short side road leads to the summit proper if you feel like doing a bit of peak bagging, although in the book the race route skips it in favor of the long, sweeping descent back to the start at Meyrueis.

ABOVE: **The meteorological observatory, built in 1893 at the summit of Mont Aigoual, is the last inhabited weather station in France.**

OPPOSITE: **The cool waters of a river valley along the Tour de Mont Aigoual**

SOUTH DOWNS WAY

Panoramic views, cathedral spires, and country pubs: a slice of old-fashioned England along one of Britain's most popular national trails

DISTANCE: **99 miles (159 km)**   SURFACE: **Off-road**   LENGTH OF TRIP: **2 to 4 days**
WHEN TO GO: **Spring through autumn**   DIFFICULTY: **Moderate to challenging**

A much loved gravel route across southern England's chalk hills, the South Downs Way links the genteel Victorian seaside holiday town of Eastbourne in East Sussex with the beautiful cathedral city of Winchester, nearly 100 miles away (161 km) in Hampshire. It is the only one of England's national scenic hiking trails that is entirely open to cyclists.

The ride starts in Eastbourne, with its old-fashioned promenade and ornate 19th-century fun pier, which has featured in many a period film and TV series. As gracious as the route's beginnings are, you soon discover that the South Downs Way is no walk in the park as you pedal your way up the flanks of the white-chalk sea cliffs that rise just west of town. Once again you find yourself in film-set country, with instantly recognizable Sussex landmarks that appear in numerous blockbusters, among them *Harry Potter and the Goblet of Fire* and *Robin Hood: Prince of Thieves;* Sussex even fills in for Gibraltar in the James Bond film *The Living Daylights.*

Once you reach the uplands, the landscape opens up spectacularly, spreading far and wide with long views over the countryside and out over the English Channel. It is startling. The empty, windswept expanses look and feel much more remote than what you'd expect to encounter in the supposedly overcrowded south of England.

It's almost like stepping into a different country. Over the next couple of days as you pedal along the trail, you amble over plenty more of this

OPPOSITE: **A cyclist pauses to take a photograph of the morning mist blanketing the South Downs near Firle, East Sussex.**

PAGES 230-31: **A mountain biker (far left) navigates verdant hills with Beachy Head Lighthouse just off the coast.**

open countryside, pass through pockets of ancient woodlands, and cross farmland dotted with sheep. Often, you drop down into picturesque villages with thatched cottages, plenty of classic country pubs offering local ales and hearty English fare, and B&Bs serving up the "full English" for breakfast.

Enjoy them. Calories don't matter. Cycling the South Downs Way is deceptively demanding, its scenic rolling landscapes involving a total of more than 12,600 feet (3,840 m) of elevation gain over the length of the trail. But it repays the effort. From the high point on the trail, the 886-foot-high (270 m) Butser Hill, in Hampshire, you can see all the way to the Isle of Wight. The trail itself is well marked and easy to follow, although take care in the wet, as the chalky clay soil can become slippery. The journey ends with a blissful descent into the beautiful medieval cathedral town of Winchester.

ARMCHAIR RIDE

The Wheels of Chance by H. G. Wells tells of young Hoopdriver, who sets off on a cycling holiday along England's south coast. Reveling in his newfound freedom, and something of a Walter Mitty, he rides to the aid of the Young Lady in Grey, a liberated upper-middle-class cyclist who is being amorously pursued by Bechamel, a caddish older cyclist. Wells, better known today as a writer of science fiction, was a keen cyclist and a shrewd observer who saw the bicycle as a vehicle for social change, female liberation, and class mobility. Wells wrote two other cycling novels: *Kipps* and *The History of Mr. Polly.*

BIRKEBEINERRITTET

A spectacular mountain bike race along the "troll tracks" that cross the mountains in central Norway—with a quirky bit of Norwegian history thrown in

DISTANCE: **53 miles (85 km)**   SURFACE: **Mainly gravel**   LENGTH OF TRIP: **I day**
WHEN TO GO: **August**   DIFFICULTY: **Moderate**

Back in A.D. 1206, during a time of violent upheaval in Norway, two loyalists managed to smuggle the infant prince Håkon, rightful heir to the throne, away from assassins who were trying to kill him. They skied swiftly through the mountains, carrying the one-year-old prince on a desperate flight to safety.

Eight centuries later their patriotic efforts are celebrated each winter with a ski race—the legendary Birkebeinerrennet—and each summer with the hugely popular mountain bike marathon Birkebeinerrittet, which takes competitors 53 miles (85 km) through these same mountains. In a delightful touch of historic verisimilitude, all contestants—from elite racers to casual weekend warriors—are obliged to carry a pack weighing 7.7 pounds (3.5 kg) to represent the weight of the baby prince. And yes, all packs are weighed before the start and spot-checked at the end, and whatever food and drink you expect to consume on the ride doesn't count toward the weight.

While not widely known outside Scandinavia, the Birkebeinerrittet is hugely loved within it, attracting almost 20,000 competitors, making it the largest MTB race in the world for sheer number of competitors. The course starts at the village of Rena and follows what Norwegians call "troll tracks," rough gravel paths and ski trails that meander through mountains and forests. It ends at Håkon's Hall in the former Olympic city of Lillehammer, where each finisher receives a medal. For those who want more of a challenge, a longer, tougher course is available: the UltraBirken, at 62 miles (100 km).

OPPOSITE: The challenging conditions don't deter devoted cyclists, who flock to Norway's Birkebeinerrittet by the thousands.

LOIRE À VÉLO

Pedal from château to château along the leafy banks
of Europe's last wild river.

DISTANCE: **560 miles (901 km)**   SURFACE: **Mainly paved**   LENGTH OF TRIP: **7 to 10 days**
WHEN TO GO: **Spring to autumn (avoid summer holidays)**   DIFFICULTY: **Easy**

Sun-drenched vineyards, magnificent châteaus, and medieval cities steeped in time—this ride along the banks of the Loire offers some of the very best of what France has to offer, whether it's food, wine, or scenery. Developed in the 1990s as an eco-friendly way to tour the wine-and-château country of the Loire Valley, the Loire à Vélo route has flourished into the longest and one of the most popular bicycle-touring routes in France.

It's not hard to see why. With hundreds of miles of easy pedaling along mainly traffic-free bicycle paths through endlessly gorgeous scenery, what's not to like? You can start the ride at either end: in the west, on the Atlantic coast where the Loire spills into the sea at the attractive old seaside resort of Saint-Brevin-les-Pins, or at its eastern terminus in the village of Cuffy, tucked away in the foothills of the Massif Central. Both starting points are easily accessible by train, as are the historic towns of Tours, Orléans, and Nantes, which lie along the route, allowing you to begin midway or ride the route in stages if you prefer.

Whichever way you travel, upstream or down, the Loire makes for a majestic riding companion. Beautiful and stately, it is said to be Europe's last wild river, having never been canalized. While it may be wild, it can make an equally valid claim to be among the continent's most civilized rivers as well. Being reasonably close to Paris, the seat of power, but set in achingly beautiful countryside with a sunny climate, the Loire Valley is where

OPPOSITE: Cycle through fragrant vineyards outside the village of Sancerre along the Loire à Vélo.

PAGES 236-37: Château de Chambord is a captivating spot for a rest stop.

the French aristocracy built their extravagant country estates and cultivated the grapes that would make this one of France's most celebrated wine regions.

It became known as the Royal River for good reason. More than 20 of these magnificent châteaus lie close to or along the route, among them the Royal Château of Amboise, the Château of Chenonceau, the Château of Azay-le-Rideau, and, the grandest of them all, Chambord, a sprawling fairy tale of 16th-century Renaissance architecture built at enormous cost as a hunting lodge for King Francis I, who spent a grand total of seven weeks there. Today the 175-mile (282 km) royal stretch of the Loire Valley between Sully-sur-Loire and Chalonnes-sur-Loire is a UNESCO World Heritage–listed landscape and a highlight of a ride along the Loire à Vélo.

CYCLING THROUGH HISTORY

Dry white wines, pungent cheeses, magnificent châteaus, and the Loire Valley itself aren't the only French cultural icons you'll encounter as you pedal from village to village. There's the humble baguette, granted heritage status by UNESCO in 2022 as part of France's "intangible cultural heritage." Baked according to strict traditions, the deliciously crusty loaf has been a vital part of French life for centuries.

ABOVE: Cyclists pause near a map of the Loire à Vélo.

OPPOSITE: A pair of cyclists cut between a river and a vineyard on the Loire à Vélo.

The path itself is a delight to ride, easy and safe, and between the châteaus and iconic towns such as Angers, Blois, and Saumur that lie along the way, it is an immersion in French history, landscape, and culture. The sole tricky part is the vast sweep of the cable-stayed Saint-Nazaire Bridge, which spans the mouth of the Loire. The bridge links together Saint-Nazaire on the north bank and Saint-Brevin-les-Pins on the south bank and is some two miles (3.2 km) long. While cyclists are allowed to cross the bridge, it's not a great idea. Happily, shuttle services and taxis exist to transport you and your bicycle across the bridge.

EL CAMINO DE SANTIAGO

Follow the centuries-old pilgrimage route across the north of Spain
to the Shrine of St. James in the cathedral of Compostela.

DISTANCE: **485 miles (780 km)**   SURFACE: **Mixed**   LENGTH OF TRIP: **2 to 3 weeks**
WHEN TO GO: **September through October**   DIFFICULTY: **Moderate**

For centuries the path to Santiago de Compostela has been a famous pilgrimage route. Traditionally, pilgrims make this journey on foot, but an increasing number are choosing to cycle.

There are many paths to Compostela, among them the Camino del Norte along Spain's northern coast; the Via de la Plata, which begins in Seville; and the Camino Frances (French Way), believed to be the oldest of the pilgrim routes.

Camino Frances starts in Saint-Jean-Pied-de-Port, a French town nestled in the foothills of the Pyrénées, and then treks through the hills across the north of Spain through Pamplona and the medieval cathedral towns of Burgos, Léon, and Astorga. While a mountain bike is preferred on the path, road bikers can easily cobble together a route.

If you are short on time or find the remote small-town starting point too difficult to reach, you can start the ride in Léon, which has good air links and is still far enough from Compostela for you to earn your pilgrim accreditation. What's more, the scenery from Léon to Compostela is arguably the prettiest, passing by the fortress towns of Palas de Rei and Sarria as you wend through the verdant Galician countryside before making a final exhilarating descent to Compostela.

OPPOSITE: Wildflowers hug a trail along El Camino de Santiago.

CANTII WAY

Canterbury Cathedral, the White Cliffs of Dover, pubs, castles, bluebells in ancient woodlands . . . Here's a chocolate-box sampler of your favorite English icons.

DISTANCE: **145 miles (233 km)**   SURFACE: **Mixed**   LENGTH OF TRIP: **3 to 5 days**
WHEN TO GO: **Early May (for the bluebells)**   DIFFICULTY: **Moderate**

You could hardly find a more quintessentially English ride than the Cantii Way, a 145-mile (233 km) loop through Kent that includes Canterbury Cathedral, the White Cliffs of Dover, fish-and-chips in gloriously tacky seaside towns, medieval castles, local ales, smugglers' coasts, old inns, oast houses, a glimpse across the water to France, and, if you time it right, the iconic carpets of bluebells in England's ancient woodlands.

Named for the Cantii—a Celtic tribe who lived in Kent during the Iron Age, and from which the town of Canterbury derives its name—the Cantii Way is one of Britain's newest long-distance cycle-touring routes. All this lies within an hour of London by train, making it possible to ride over a long weekend or, with so many towns along it accessible by rail, to do it in stages. The riding is along traffic-free bicycle paths, farm tracks, bridleways, and quiet country lanes, and although the route is not yet signposted specifically as the Cantii Way, it follows a succession of well-marked National Cycle Network routes for which maps and GPS guidance are available.

The starting point is the medieval village of Wye, in the heart of what's known as the Garden of England, a rolling patchwork of field and forest brightened in the springtime with dazzling yellow crops of rapeseed. Pedaling north through the hills toward Canterbury, 14 miles (22 km) away, you pass through King's Wood, which from late April through early May is carpeted with iconic bluebells.

OPPOSITE: Quaint houses and a haunted inn on Mermaid Street in historic Rye, East Sussex

PAGES 244-45: Cyclists head for the Folkestone Harbour Arm in Kent, a great rest stop along the Cantii Way.

Canterbury announces itself with a glimpse of its famous cathedral spires rising in the distance. A pilgrimage site since before Chaucer's day, its 11th-century cathedral is one of three UNESCO World Heritage–listed structures in the history-rich town, the others being the sixth-century St. Martin's Church and the equally ancient St. Augustine's Abbey. The Cantii Way guides you into the heart of the city with minimal fuss and back into the countryside, continuing north for almost eight miles (13 km) to Whitstable, an attractive seaside town that overlooks the Thames estuary and is famous for its oysters.

From here the ride follows nearly the whole of the Kent coast through raffish old seaside towns with Victorian fun piers and stalls selling jellied eels, cockles and mussels, bright plastic beach toys, fish-and-chips, sticks of peppermint rock, and tacky postcards. It's easy pedaling until you come around to Folkestone and Dover and those famous white cliffs. Here the path climbs steeply to the cliff tops, with stunning views over the English Channel to the French coast some 20 miles (32 km) away.

ARMCHAIR RIDE

Every summer between 1924 and 1933, a middle-age London law clerk named Charles Pope went on a cycling tour through the English and Welsh countrysides. The diary he kept of these journeys was discovered a few years ago in a box of old books bought at auction and turned into the beloved *A Golden Age of Cycling*. Charming and highly readable, it opens a delightful window into British cycling. It's the perfect armchair read for a cycling romantic.

Then it's back down again for a nearly dead-level run along the southern coast, past the vast beach at Camber Sands, and on into the ancient seafaring town of Rye, one of the original Cinque Ports—a select group of towns that provided ships for the navy during the Middle Ages in return for lucrative trading privileges. Much later, during the 18th century, Rye was a hotbed of smuggling, and so open about it that the 700-year-old Mermaid Inn was said to be a no-go area for revenue officers who wanted to stay healthy. Now the landmark pub is a great spot to grab a meal or a pint of local ale, or to reserve as a bed-and-breakfast if you want to end your journey on a historical high. Queen Elizabeth I also stayed here when she passed through Rye in 1573. From here it's an easy jaunt by bike or train to complete the loop back to your starting point.

CANAL DU MIDI

Follow the towpath of a World Heritage–listed 17th-century canal as it makes its way from Toulouse to the Mediterranean.

DISTANCE: **184 miles (296 km)**   SURFACE: **Varied**   LENGTH OF TRIP: **3 to 5 days**
WHEN TO GO: **Summer**   DIFFICULTY: **Moderate**

S omething of a hidden diamond in the rough, the Canal du Midi cycle route follows the line of Europe's oldest canal as it meanders across the South of France from Toulouse to the port city of Sète on the Mediterranean coast.

The UNESCO World Heritage–listed canal was completed in 1681 and was considered an engineering marvel of its time, being the first in the world to use locks to raise and lower boats as they traveled along its length, an idea originally conceived by Leonardo da Vinci, who more than 150 years earlier was commissioned by King Francis I to study the possibility of one day building just such a canal.

The brilliance of the design and the aesthetics of the waterway itself (in the way it follows the contours of the landscape) caught the eye of Thomas Jefferson when he traveled it in 1787. "Of all the methods of travelling I have ever tried this is the pleasantest," he wrote in a letter to a friend. "I walk the greater part of the way along the banks of the canal, level, and lined with a double row of trees which furnish shade."

Centuries later the Canal du Midi is still a beautiful waterway, although these days some of the stretches of the towpath along its banks are better suited to mountain biking than a gentlemanly stroll. With horses no longer

OPPOSITE: A cyclist enjoys a misty sunrise on the Canal du Midi channel in Argens-Minervois.

PAGES 250-51: A row of bikes await their destination in the town of Béziers on the Canal du Midi.

pulling barges down the canal, the unpaved towpath beside it has become overgrown in places. Conditions vary greatly, from smooth and delightful to rough and challenging. Happily, there are plenty of quiet backroads on which to detour around these rough patches. Certainly the scenery and history repay the effort. Pick up the trail on the Garonne River in the heart of Toulouse—known as "the Rose City" because of the pink terra-cotta bricks used in so much of its architecture—and follow it out of town, to the medieval city of Carcassonne some 60 miles (97 km) away and on through the wine country of southern France to the shores of the Mediterranean.

PHOTO OP

Perched amid the clouds atop a verdant hill, the city of Carcassonne is a can't-miss photo opportunity. With 52 towers, it's the largest citadel in Europe and a spectacular sight. Also worthy of your lens are the charming cobbled streets, bustling food market, and awe-inspiring views from the walls.

APPLECROSS LOOP

Hills and heather on a remote peninsula in the Scottish Highlands

DISTANCE: **43 miles (69 km)**   SURFACE: **Paved**   LENGTH OF TRIP: **1 day**
WHEN TO GO: **Spring and autumn (avoid the summer holidays)**   DIFFICULTY: **Challenging**

A wild and rugged peninsula in one of the more remote pockets of the Scottish Highlands, Applecross offers cyclists not only splendid isolation and dramatic scenery but also a glorious challenge pedaling Bealach na Bà (Pass of the Cattle), widely regarded as one of the toughest and yet most beautiful climbs in Britain.

The road over the mountain pass was built in 1822, and as with those roads over the continent's great alpine passes, which it closely resembles, Bealach na Bà makes the ascent in a series of tight hairpins and switchbacks. Starting from sea level and climbing more than 2,000 feet (610 m), with gradients approaching 20 percent, it has the highest elevation gain of any road in Britain. Conquering it is a bucket-list aspiration among British road cyclists, since it is not only steep but also, with nearly six miles (9.6 km) at an average grade of about 7 percent, the nearest thing in Britain to ascending one of the legendary passes in the Alps.

The climb is beautiful as well, the high point of a hauntingly desolate loop of hills and heather around the Applecross Peninsula with stunning views to the Isle of Skye. Start at the village of Applecross, on the outer part of the peninsula, and ride in a counterclockwise direction, saving the climb for the end of the ride so that you can enjoy the fast, curvy descent back to where you started.

BREAKOUT

The Applecross Peninsula lies just off a spectacular 500-mile (805 km) loop around the Scottish Highlands. Regarded as one of the world's great road trips, it can also be a wonderful long-distance route—but go in the off-season, autumn or spring. The NC500 receives a lot of tourist traffic during the summer.

OPPOSITE: Ascending a hill on the singletrack road Bealach na Bà in the Applecross Peninsula of Wester Ross in the Scottish Highlands

ROMANTIC ROAD

The name says it all: a magical ride through a baroque landscape of vineyards with picturesque churches and fairy-tale castles.

DISTANCE: **286 miles (460 km)**   SURFACE: **Mixed**   LENGTH OF TRIP: **7 to 10 days**
WHEN TO GO: **Late spring or early autumn (avoid the summer crowds)**   DIFFICULTY: **Easy to moderate**

Meandering through vineyards and quaint river valleys from the restored medieval town of Würzburg in the north to the fairy-tale castle of Neuschwanstein in the south, Germany's aptly named Romantic Road is a rolling cavalcade of some of Europe's most romantic landscapes, scenes, and settings.

Originally conceived as a motoring route in the 1950s, it has become hugely popular among cyclists. As a result, one of Germany's great long-distance bicycle touring routes—the D9 Weser—shadows the motoring version closely on quiet backroads and traffic-free bicycle paths.

The Romantic Road can be ridden from either end, although most choose to ride north to south, allowing for a slow, more dramatic buildup to the finish at the foothills of the Alps. As is usually the case with Germany's main cycle touring routes, an excellent guidebook is available: Bikeline's *Romantische Strasse,* with easy-to-read large-scale maps specifically designed for cyclists, plenty of information (albeit in German), and a perfect size to fit in a handlebar bag.

Pick up the cycle path by the Marienberg Fortress, a massive 17th-century baroque structure that occupies a hilltop on the opposite bank of the Main River from Würzburg's city center. From Würzburg, the Romantic Road

OPPOSITE: The scenery of the Romantic Road lives up to its name, including Germany's 19th-century Hohenschwangau Castle.

PAGES 256-57: Cyclists make their way along a cobblestone street in the historic town of Füssen.

leads you from castle town to castle town through the vineyards of the Franconian wine district before joining the Tauber River and following its lovely valley upstream to the beautiful medieval walled town Rothenburg ob der Tauber, famed for its storybook architecture.

A few miles upstream, the town of Nördlingen is equally as beautiful and has the distinction of being among the very few German towns whose complete medieval walls are still standing. If these two fairy-tale towns seem oddly familiar, it's because you may well have seen them before: Magical-looking Rothenburg provided the inspiration for the village in Disney's *Pinocchio*. An aerial shot over Nördlingen was used in *Willy Wonka & the Chocolate Factory* (1971).

As you continue south, the countryside becomes progressively more rolling and hilly—you're in Bavarian beer country now. You cross the Danube at Donauwörth and from there pass a succession of quaint towns, baroque churches, monasteries, and castles, until the Romantic Road reaches its crescendo in the form of the fairy-tale Neuschwanstein Castle. Built in 1869, the castle provides a fitting end to a ride through one of Europe's most magical landscapes.

RING OF KERRY

Explore Ireland's wild, rugged, and remote Iveragh Peninsula.

DISTANCE: **134 miles (216 km)**   SURFACE: **Paved**   LENGTH OF TRIP: **1 to 3 days**
WHEN TO GO: **Spring through autumn**   DIFFICULTY: **Moderate**

The Iveragh Peninsula in County Kerry is one of the most beautiful places in Ireland. Located on the wild and rugged southwest coast, with a spine of mountains along its length and traced by narrow winding roads, it is a fabulous place to explore by bicycle. Indeed, riding the Ring of Kerry, as the bike route around the peninsula is called, is one of Ireland's most popular one-day cycling events, held each summer, with thousands tackling a 105-mile (169 km) loop of the peninsula.

If events aren't your thing or the timing isn't right, the lovely scenery and roads are there year-round. At 134 miles (216 km), the touring loop is longer than that used in the cycling event, keeps to quieter roads, and meanders out to Valentia Island, one of the westernmost parts of Ireland. It starts and ends in Killarney and is best ridden clockwise. Highlights are the 15th-century Ross Castle, the Torc Waterfall in Killarney National Park, the Iron Age fort at Cahergall, and the lovely view across Dingle Bay from the little fishing village of Kells. Take a boat eight miles (12.9 km) out from Portmagee to Skellig Michael, a hauntingly desolate splinter of rock more than 700 feet (215 m) high on which a dozen reclusive monks of the order of St. Fionán built a simple monastery in the sixth century A.D. *Star Wars* fans will know that Skellig Michael was also where scenes from *Star Wars: The Force Awakens* and *Star Wars: The Last Jedi* were filmed.

It isn't only cyclists who are drawn to the wild and beautiful Ring of Kerry; it's a popular drive as well. The roads are narrow, so avoid the peak summer season. Bring your rain gear, and be prepared for fickle weather. There's a reason Ireland is so green.

OPPOSITE: **A biker makes a quick descent among the craggy hills of Ballaghbeama Gap in County Kerry.**

PARIS-ROUBAIX

Test your mettle on the legendary cobbled roads of Paris-Roubaix, made famous by the tough 125-year-old race.

DISTANCE: **66 miles (106 km)**   SURFACE: **Paved, with long stretches of cobbles**
LENGTH OF TRIP: **1 day**   WHEN TO GO: **Spring**   DIFFICULTY: **Challenging**

One of the oldest races in the pro-cycling calendar (dating from 1896), Paris-Roubaix is widely regarded as one of the toughest as well. It's a one-day race, one of the so-called Spring Classics, held around Easter Sunday, more often than not in atrocious weather. Racers compete on a brutal 160-mile (257 km) course in northern France that includes long stretches of steep, treacherous cobbles that can break bicycles and bodies—and make or break careers.

Nicknamed the "Hell of the North," Paris-Roubaix is one of cycling's most storied races too, with each edition packed with drama, crashes, and heroism. And it's the subject of the award-winning 1976 documentary *A Sunday in Hell*.

For those who want to experience some of the challenges of this legendary race, gaining an appreciation for the skill and courage involved without the speed and terror of actual racing, this sampler includes 18 of the race's most iconic cobbled sections—the ride's greatest hits, so to speak, including the most famous of them all: the Trouée d'Arenberg, a mile-and-a-half-long (2.4 km) stretch of vicious cobbles along a dead-straight Napoleonic-era road that climbs through the Arenberg Forest.

Although the race is called Paris-Roubaix, since 1977 the starting line has actually been in Compiègne, which is some 55 miles (89 km) northeast of the city. This taster of a ride picks up in the village of Haveluy, at a point where the pros would have already been on the road for roughly 87 miles

OPPOSITE: A group of cyclists push through dusty conditions as they compete in the 119th Paris-Roubaix.

PAGES 262-63: A cloud of dust trails a pack of cyclists rounding a bend during the race.

(140 km), and takes you all the way to the end, at the velodrome at Roubaix on the Belgian border, some 66 miles (106 km) away.

Up to this point the race unfolded mainly on normal roads; here is where all the glamorous danger begins. Straightaway, you're into the action with a section of cobbles, but this is merely the warm-up for what follows soon after: the Trouée d'Arenberg, first of the three five-star-rated cobble stretches along the route. Forget any notion you may have of egg-smooth cobbles. These are chunky, bone-juddering lumps on which it is alarmingly easy to catch a rim and flip yourself over the handlebars.

The trick to riding pavé, say the pros, is to hold your handlebars loosely, shift your weight toward the back of the bike, and pedal briskly—never coast! Aim for the crown of the road if you can; this will offer you the smoothest, safest riding.

ARMCHAIR RIDE

Too wet and muddy outside to go for a spin yourself? Then settle into your armchair and spend an absorbing couple of hours watching others get muddied, bloodied, and bedraggled on the cobbles of northern France in the iconic documentary *A Sunday in Hell.* In 1976 Danish director Jørgen Leth produced this 111-minute documentary about that year's edition of the famously brutal Paris-Roubaix one-day race, known as the Hell of the North. In it, he interviews racers, mechanics, and spectators, and vividly captures the atmosphere of the event.

As you pedal, be grateful for the luxury of having the road to yourself. Imagine doing all this at high speed, in wind and rain, elbowing your way through a frenetic peloton of fellow racers who, like you, all want the center of the road.

And to think: After the Trouée d'Arenberg you still have another 16 segments of cobbles to go, most of them rated three or four stars on the difficulty and danger scale, and two of them—Mons-en-Pévèle and Carrefour de l'Arbre—given the scariest five-star rating. By the time you finish your white-knuckle ride into Roubaix, rolling on smooth pavement will never have felt so good.

And yet you might find yourself thinking how you'll handle those cobbles *next* time, for as many a Spring Classics racer can tell you, the challenge of riding the rough muddy pavé of northern France can be highly addictive.

GAVIA-MORTIROLO LOOP

A stunning climb over two of Italian road cycling's most iconic mountain passes

DISTANCE: **70 miles (113 km)**   SURFACE: **Paved**   LENGTH OF TRIP: **1 day**
WHEN TO GO: **June through September**   DIFFICULTY: **Challenging**

A *Beauty and the Beast*–like pairing, this spectacular loop combines two mountain passes—Passo di Gavia and Passo del Mortirolo, both famous in Italy's road cycling circles—into a single dramatic ride that encompasses the high-Alpine beauty of the Gavia with the brutally steep beast of a road up the Mortirolo.

The ride sets off from Bormio, heading south, with an easy warm-up along the beautiful Valtellina Valley, through the medieval town of Grosio and on to Mazzo di Valtellina and the start of the climb up the Mortirolo. From here the road rears up sharply, and you see why the Mortirolo—whose name derives from Italian for "death"—earned its reputation among professional cyclists (Lance Armstrong once described this climb as the toughest he'd ever ridden). For the next 7.7 miles (12.4 km), through 32 switchback turns, the twisting, narrow road creeps up the mountainside at an average gradient of 10.5 percent, spiking to more than 18 percent in places.

Once above the tree line, still climbing steeply, you pass a stone memorial to the late Marco Pantani, the brilliant but flawed Italian cyclist who launched a blistering attack on the slopes of the Mortirolo during the 1994 Giro d'Italia, cresting the 6,076-foot (1,852 m) pass ahead of the peloton and cementing himself as a cycling legend by completing the climb in an astonishing 42:40—to this day one of the fastest-ever ascents.

OPPOSITE: The medieval town of Bormio is a popular spot for skiing and cycling alike.

PAGES 268-69: Located on the road to the Mortirolo Pass, the stunning Church of the Blessed Virgin of Pompeii was built between 1888 and 1897.

The descent from the Mortirolo is steep and curvy, dropping down to the village of Monno for a brief section of flattish riding before the ascent of the higher and more scenic Gavia, at 8,599 feet (2,621 m), one of the highest passes in the Italian Alps. It's a different sort climb to the Mortirolo—longer, quieter, not as brutally steep, as it emerges onto a barren landscape of rock and moss at about 6,076 feet (1,852 m) with spectacular views over the valleys below.

With two miles (3.2 km) of climbing still to go, you come to Gavia's notorious tunnel, a narrow, unlit passage that climbs steeply for several hundred yards; you'll want lights if you plan to tackle the tunnel. A more scenic alternative is to take the old cliff road. It is gravel in places, but many prefer it, even if they have to walk.

The final two miles (3.2 km) to the summit are steep and exposed. Bear in mind that the weather at this altitude can be wintry, even in summer. The descent back to Bormio is beautiful: miles of sweeping, plunging curves with stunning views of the Italian Alps.

ALTERNATE ROUTE

If you want to round out your Italian Alpine experience, there is always the legendary Stelvio, at 9,045 feet (2,757 m), the highest paved pass in the Italian Alps. It's famed among cycling romantics as the setting where Italian hero Fausto Coppi beat the Swiss great Hugo Koblet to the top during the 1953 Giro d'Italia. On Bike Day, held each August, thousands of cyclists make the ascent.

CAP DE FORMENTOR

Jaw-dropping views of the Mediterranean await along this out-and-back ride to an old lighthouse on the wild and dramatic Majorcan coast.

DISTANCE: **25 miles (40 km)**   SURFACE: **Paved**   LENGTH OF TRIP: **I day**
WHEN TO GO: **Spring; early morning is best**   DIFFICULTY: **Moderate**

With its predictable sunshine, quiet roads, and mix of punchy climbs and long, flat stretches, Majorca has been a honeypot for pro racers, whose teams come here to train for races such as the Tour de France. If you time your visit for the spring, you're likely to encounter more than a few mini-pelotons of pros and amateur teams putting themselves through their paces ahead of the coming season.

One of the loveliest rides you can undertake on the island is this out-and-back jaunt to the Formentor Lighthouse, the highest lighthouse in the Balearic Islands at the northernmost tip of Majorca. Starting in the town of Puerto Pollensa, you head north for a brisk warm-up climb along the Coll de Sa Creueta, with its hairpin bends and postcard views over the Tramuntana Mountains, and Majorca's wild coastline and the azure blue Mediterranean spreading away below. A breezy descent takes you back to the coast at Formentor beach. Follow this up with a rolling climb through a forest of Mediterranean pines and along sheer cliffs out to the lighthouse, which sits atop a dramatic rocky headland some 700 feet (215 m) above the sea. The views are jaw-dropping. What's more, you'll see them all a second time on the homeward leg back to Pollensa.

OPPOSITE: Bikers ride the curve on the Balearic Islands in Majorca, Spain.

COL DU TOURMALET

Rise to the challenge of conquering the most iconic mountain pass in the Tour de France.

DISTANCE: 22 miles (35 km)   **SURFACE:** Paved   **LENGTH OF TRIP:** 1 day
WHEN TO GO: June through September   **DIFFICULTY:** Challenging

"Assassins!" roared Octave Lapize at the tour organizers who stood atop the Col du Tourmalet watching the shattered young rider crest the pass on a sultry July afternoon during the 1910 Tour de France. It was the first time the race had ventured into the mountains. At 6,939 feet (2,115 m), the remote Col du Tourmalet was higher than any professional race had ever gone before. Until a few weeks earlier, there had been no road over the pass, only a centuries-old goat track. When a race organizer scouted the route earlier that May, he found the pass blocked by deep snow and local guides reluctant to accompany him. With the help of a shepherd, he succeeded in climbing the pass on foot but fell on the descent, tumbling into an icy stream from which he had to be rescued and suffering severe hypothermia. Nevertheless, once back in town, he telegraphed his superiors in Paris to say that the route over the Tourmalet was perfectly acceptable for cycling—then slipped local authorities 3,000 francs to widen the existing goat track and hoped for the best.

Thankfully no bandits, bears, or snowdrifts blighted the climb, but race leader Lapize found himself obliged to push up some of the steeper, more gravelly bits, and by the time he reached the top, he was outraged that anyone could possibly have thought this was a good idea. And yet it was.

OPPOSITE: A breathtaking view of the setting for the Col du Tourmalet

PAGES 274-75: Riders pause for photos in front of a statue of French cycling legend Octave Lapize at the top of the Col du Tourmalet.

Over the coming decades, this frequently revisited climb through the high Pyrénées became an iconic part of Tour de France history and a must-do ride on the bucket lists of road-racing romantics everywhere.

You can start your ascent on either side of the pass, but Luz-Saint-Sauveur, on the western side, is a particularly vivacious town in which to base yourself and is within easy striking distance of some of the tour's other legendary mountain passes—icons such as the Hautacam, Col de Peyresourde, Col du Portet, and Col d'Aubisque.

From Luz it is a little more than 12 miles (19 km) to the top of the Tourmalet. The first few miles are relatively easy. The road out of town is wide, with long straightaways and steady gradients. The first hairpin switchback you come to is just below the village of Barèges. From here the road becomes steeper, more exposed, and narrower. The last two miles (3.2 km) before the top are the toughest,

BREAKOUT

The Tourmalet may be the star climb of the French Pyrénées, steeped in history and mystique, but the nearby Col d'Aubisque runs a close second and is breathtakingly beautiful. Like the Tourmalet, the Col d'Aubisque first appeared in the 1910 edition of the Tour de France and has featured regularly in the race ever since. Start at the village of Argelès-Gazost, make your ascent via the lovely Col du Soulor, and then drop back down the other side of the pass into the old spa town of Eaux-Bonnes. The scenery and mountain views along the way are spectacular.

ABOVE: A herd of llamas perch at the edge of the road on the Col du Tourmalet.

OPPOSITE: A trio of bikers on the road up the Col du Tourmalet in the Pyrénées mountains

a series of grueling hairpins at a pitiless 12 percent grade, but the views of the valley are stunning. The distant tinkle of cowbells in the still mountain air enhances the sense of remoteness. The old café at the top of the pass is a welcome sight.

The descent down the eastern flank is swift and curvy, dropping into shady forests and passing through two tunnels on your way to Sainte-Marie-de-Campan. Spare a thought for Eugène Christophe, an indomitable French rider who was leading the 1913 Tour de France when his front fork snapped on this descent. Weeping with frustration, he grabbed his broken bicycle and ran with it for six miles (9.6 km) down the mountain to Sainte-Marie-de-Campan, where he borrowed the local blacksmith's forge, mended the fork on his bike, refitted it, and pedaled away for all he was worth, having lost three hours to his rival but refusing to yield.

RALLARVEGEN

Explore Norway's grandest fjord on this old and nearly traffic-free railway access road.

DISTANCE: **51 miles (82 km)**   SURFACE: **Mixed**   LENGTH OF TRIP: **1 day**
WHEN TO GO: **July through September**   DIFFICULTY: **Moderate**

E ven in a country as renowned for gorgeous scenery as Norway, the Rallarvegen is something special. Widely regarded as the country's most spectacular bicycle ride, it takes you from the high glacier-clad mountains along the coast down to a picturesque village on the shores of Norway's most dramatic fjord.

It follows an old access track, built between 1902 and 1904 for workers involved in the construction of the Oslo-Bergen railway line. The ride starts at Haugastøl, accessible by train from either Bergen or Oslo. For the first 17 miles (27 km) or so, you climb through beautiful alpine moorland to the town of Finse—also accessible by rail if you prefer a shorter journey.

At Finse the trail continues into Hardangervidda National Park to Lake Fagervatnet, which, at 4,406 feet (1,343 m), is the highest point along the track. Even in summer you may encounter snow.

From the lake, however, it is virtually all downhill. The road narrows, and the landscape shifts from the high moorland of the mountains to the wilder, more Tolkienesque scenery of the fjord. The going can be rough, with the track often in poor condition, so take care on the 21 hairpin turns on the descent. You'll want to pause frequently to take in the views of the lush fjord-land scenery, waterfalls, and rushing rivers. Sognefjord, into which you're descending, is known as the King of Fjords for its grandeur. At the bottom is the village of Flåm, the end of your ride. From here you can take the Flåm railway—one of the world's most scenic railway journeys—to Myrdal, on the Bergen–Oslo line, and your train back to the city.

OPPOSITE: **The Rallarvegen trail runs along roaring Flåmselvi River in the lush Flåmsdalen Valley.**

FRED WHITTON CHALLENGE

Tackle some of Britain's steepest country lanes on this jaw-droppingly beautiful ride through Wordsworth's Lake District.

DISTANCE: 112 miles (180 km)   **SURFACE: Paved**   **LENGTH OF TRIP: 1 day**
WHEN TO GO: Spring through autumn   **DIFFICULTY: Extreme**

E
ngland's Lake District may be Wordsworth Country in the minds of many. But among cyclists the region is famed for its extraordinarily steep climbs, some of them with gradients exceeding 30 percent, and for the Fred Whitton Challenge, the toughest cycling event in Britain, yet one of the most popular.

Named in memory of the secretary of a local bicycle club who died in 1998, the Fred Whitton Challenge is a one-day sportive charity-raising event that collects the Lake District's steepest climbs into a single glorious 112-mile (180 km) loop. Here you can bag all of British cycling's most famous cols—Hardknott, Wrynose, Keswick, Newlands, Honister, Cold Fell, and the Struggle to Kirkstone Pass—any one of which would be considered a bucket-list climb on its own. Perhaps the only thing tougher than completing the Fred Whitton Challenge is getting an entry. Numbers are limited and entry is by ballot; it is always heavily oversubscribed.

Happily, the roads are open to the public and rideable anytime, so if you can't get a slot on the day or would rather do it on your own, you can still ride the Fred Whitton loop—and better still, take a couple of days to do it, since this is one of the most beautiful pockets of Britain. There are definite advantages to doing this as a DIY ride: It can be stressful spinning down some

OPPOSITE: Racers ascend the steep ramp of Hard-knott Pass in the English Lake District.

PAGES 282-83: A lone cyclist winds through Cheddar Gorge in the Mendip Hills of Somerset.

280   100 BIKE RIDES OF A LIFETIME

of those harrowing descents in the company of hundreds of riders of widely varying abilities.

The loop starts and ends in Grasmere. Kirkstone Pass is the first of the tough climbs, barely 11 miles (18 km) into your ride. At 1,489 feet (454 m), it's the highest pass in England, and as you churn your way up, you'll understand why the road is known as the Struggle. But at a mere 17 percent grade, Kirkstone is just the warm-up for the monster grades to come. The pièce de résistance is Hardknott Pass, at the 94-mile (151 km) point in the ride, its 30 percent gradient so steep that if you don't lean out over the handlebars as you ascend, you could flip over backward.

The descents are every bit as challenging—but far scarier and more treacherous, and just as likely to make you want to dismount. The lumpy roads down Keswick and Honister Passes require particular care. But there is more than just bragging rights for knocking off the toughest climbs in the country. This is one of the most beautiful parts of Britain, and the sweeping views are unforgettable.

ALTERNATE ROUTE

A quieter and shorter ride through the Lake District can be had on the 40-mile (64 km) Lakeland Loop. Beginning and ending in Lowick, it starts off with a spin along the shores of Coniston Water, with lovely views across the lake heading into the hills. The loop includes an ascent up the notorious Wrynose Pass, whose 30 percent grade won't leave you feeling shortchanged.

SOUTHERN BLACK FOREST CYCLE ROUTE

Explore a storybook landscape of dark woods, deep gorges, and medieval castles.

DISTANCE: 149 miles (240 km)   **SURFACE:** Paved   **LENGTH OF TRIP:** 3 to 5 days
WHEN TO GO: Spring through autumn   **DIFFICULTY:** Easy

A dark magical wood famed for cherry-topped chocolate cake and as the inspiration for the brothers Grimm's collection of fairy tales, Germany's Black Forest is a perfect place to explore by bicycle. This easy-to-pedal 149-mile (240 km) loop through its southern reaches along the Swiss border not only takes you through some of the prettiest sections of the Schwarzwald but also avoids most of the hilly bits along the way.

The journey starts in beautiful Freiburg, an old university town whose cobbled streets and half-timbered storybook architecture helps set the tone for the ride. Pedaling east, following the route in a clockwise direction, you soon come to the only genuinely hilly portion of the ride as the route winds through Hell's Valley, so named because early travelers heading up this dark, steep-walled gorge felt as though they were underground. If you prefer to spare yourself the climb, the train between Kirchzarten and Hinterzarten is a popular alternative.

From Hinterzarten, the route ambles through the forest, passes beautiful Lake Titisee and old castle towns, heads south to hug the Swiss border, and then nips into Basel before going north again to close the loop at Freiburg.

ARMCHAIR RIDE

Though written in 1900, *Three Men on the Bummel,* English satirist Jerome K. Jerome's humorous take on bicycle saddles, maintenance, and the uselessness of foreign-language phrase books, still brings smiles to globe-trotting cyclists today.

OPPOSITE: Picturesque fields and verdant vineyards make up the landscapes along the Southern Black Forest Cycle Route.

WEST LOOP

This backwoods bikepacking adventure in the heart of central Europe has it all, from medieval castles to wild mountain streams to the chance of encountering a bear.

DISTANCE: **260 miles (418 km)**   SURFACE: **Varied**   LENGTH OF TRIP: **6 to 8 days**
WHEN TO GO: **August through September**   DIFFICULTY: **Moderate to challenging**

Tucked away in the forests of central Europe, tiny Slovenia is an undiscovered gem, packing an astonishing array of unspoiled travel-poster landscapes—Alps, vineyards, storybook castles, picturesque villages, deep forests, wild rivers, and pristine lakes—into an area scarcely larger than the state of New Jersey.

Cycling is popular here. And with more than half the country covered by forest—Slovenia is one of the greenest places in Europe and holds the continent's record for carbon dioxide absorption, with its forests absorbing nine metric tons of CO_2 per hectare per year—some great bikepacking possibilities are on offer. Among the best is the West Loop trail, a mainly gravel ride that makes a circuit of the country's wild and remote northwest.

Starting and ending in the country's pretty capital city, Ljubljana, the trail takes in many of Slovenia's most beautiful attractions, including Lake Bled, Predjama Castle, the Julian Alps, and Triglav National Park. It follows the turquoise waters of the Soča River along its beautiful valley, crosses the historic Vršič Pass on old World War I roads with overgrown bunkers and gun emplacements still visible, and nips briefly into Italy as you head back toward Ljubljana.

It's not an easy circuit—more than 29,000 feet (8,840 m) of climbing is involved—and riding surfaces vary from smooth pavement to cobblestones

OPPOSITE: Slovenia's Vršič Pass is the highest mountain pass in the eastern Julian Alps, tucked amid Triglav National Park.

PAGES 288-89: Lake Bled has the only natural island in Slovenia, which is home to the 17th-century Assumption of Mary Church.

to dirt roads to challenging sections of singletrack. Heavily wooded, mountainous Slovenia is one of the last places where all three of Europe's big predators (brown bears, wolves, and lynx) still roam wild. It has one of Europe's biggest populations of brown bears; you'll see signs warning you to be on the lookout. The bear population has been growing strongly in recent years and is now estimated at 1,000 animals. (Bear-spotting safaris are available.) But that's part of the adventure.

ALTERNATE ROUTE

For a shorter adventure in Slovenia, try the new Green Capitals Route. Opened in October 2020, the 108-mile-long (174 km) route is like a sampler of the best of what Slovenia has to offer, linking its cosmopolitan capital city, Ljubljana, with Kočevsko, in the heart of the World Heritage–listed Kočevsko primeval forest, and then with the cultural capital of Bela Krajina, renowned for its food and wine. All three cities are linked by rail, making it easy to do as an out-and-back ride.

CORSICAN COAST

Picturesque villages, craggy mountains, narrow roads, and wild coastlines await along this hidden gem of an island in the Mediterranean.

DISTANCE: **56 miles (90 km)**   SURFACE: **Paved, but rough in places**   LENGTH OF TRIP: **1 to 2 days**
WHEN TO GO: **Spring through autumn (avoid August holidays)**   DIFFICULTY: **Challenging**

Corsica is a hidden gem for cyclists. Its combination of craggy mountains, narrow twisting roads, and dramatic Mediterranean coastline makes for some of the most exhilarating riding anywhere. While the possibilities for exploring Corsica by bike are endless, this loop through the mountains and along the coast in the northwest corner of the island is among the best.

The ride starts in Calvi, a lovely town perched on a rocky headland overlooking the sea, and heads south, twisting and writhing its way into the hills and along a wild and staggeringly beautiful coastline. The approach to Porto is especially stunning, with the road clinging improbably to the dramatic ocher red cliffs that line this part of the coast. The secluded seaside town, overlooking the Golfo de Porto, makes a nice place to stop for lunch before tackling the final few miles.

From Porto, the road climbs steeply through one of the highlights of the ride: the Calanques de Piana, an otherworldly landscape of limestone formations carved by nature into scores of strange shapes. It makes for a spectacular finale. The climb brings you to Piana, a village regarded as one of the most beautiful in France, perched some 1,444 feet (440 m) above the sea, giving you sweeping views over the cliffs and dramatic Mediterranean coast along which you've just ridden.

OPPOSITE: **A mountain biker takes a break on the coast of Bonifacio in Corsica, France.**

WAY OF THE ROSES

Tudor history and achingly beautiful northern English landscapes on a coast-to-coast ride brimming with history

DISTANCE: 171 miles (275 km)   SURFACE: Varied   LENGTH OF TRIP: 3 to 5 days
WHEN TO GO: Spring through autumn   DIFFICULTY: Moderate

Named after the long-running civil war between Britain's two rival royal dynasties in the 15th century—the House of Lancaster, whose emblem was the red rose, and the House of York, whose heraldic rose was white—the Way of the Roses is a spectacular coast-to-coast cycle route across the north of England connecting the historic cities of Lancaster and York and passing through the Pennines and stunningly beautiful Yorkshire Dales National Park.

Running mainly on quiet backroads and leafy country lanes, with a short, easy-to-pedal rails-to-trails stretch, the Way of the Roses starts at the seafront in Morecambe, west of Lancaster, then rolls across miles of achingly beautiful northern English countryside and through the ancient cathedral city of York to finish up on the coast at Bridlington. The route is well marked, with signs emblazoned with red and white heraldic roses.

Tradition holds that before you start, you walk your bike down to the tide line at Morecambe and dip your rear wheel in the waters of the Irish Sea so that when you reach the North Sea on the coast of Yorkshire, 171 miles (275 km) away, you can fairly say you've ridden sea to sea.

The first few miles are deceptively easy, along a traffic-free cycle path following an abandoned railway bed through the Victorian industrial city of Lancaster and into the picturesque River Lune Valley.

OPPOSITE: The historic village of Burnsall, once an Anglo-Viking settlement, sits on the River Wharfe on the Way of the Roses route.

PAGES 294-95: The Way of the Roses passes through the Yorkshire Dales upland area, including Yorkshire Dales National Park.

The hills soon rise up. While English hills might not be terribly high or terribly long, they are steep. The cobbled climb out of the ancient market town of Settle, about 30 miles (48 km) east of Lancaster, on High Hill Lane is a heart-stopping 25 percent grade, but the scenery spreading out before you eastward amply repays the effort, offering stunning views over Yorkshire's three famous peaks: Ingleborough, Pen-y-ghent, and Whernside.

Over the next couple of days, you pass though the hauntingly beautiful Yorkshire Dales, the Vale of York, and the Yorkshire Wolds, along with a succession of historic market towns and the beautifully preserved medieval city of York, with its magnificent 13th-century cathedral, one of the biggest in northern Europe and with more medieval stained glass than any other cathedral in Britain. The final 34 miles (55 km) of the ride, east of York, take you to the seaside resort of Bridlington, where you can wheel your bike across the beach to dip your front tire in the chilly waters of the North Sea.

BREAKOUT

The north of England has an embarrassment of riches when it comes to scenic coast-to-coast cycle routes. In addition to the Way of the Roses, there is the classic 137-mile-long (220 km) C2C route from the Cumbrian coast to Tyneside, on the North Sea; and the 170-mile (274 km) Hadrian's Cycleway, which broadly follows the ruins of the Roman-era Hadrian's Wall across Cumbria and Northumberland to Newcastle.

ÎLE DE RÉ

Discover this secluded, cycle-friendly gem of an island off the west coast of France.

DISTANCE: **37 miles (60 km)**   SURFACE: **Paved**   LENGTH OF TRIP: **I day**
WHEN TO GO: **May through mid-July or September through October**   DIFFICULTY: **Easy**

A gem of an island off the west coast of France, and quiet for much of the year, the Île de Ré has long been a popular getaway for Parisians in the know. With few cars, picturesque villages, and lovely coastal scenery, the 19-mile-long (31 km) island is a haven for cyclists. More than 60 miles (97 km) of largely traffic-free bicycle routes crisscross the island, offering plenty of family-friendly touring.

One of the nicest routes is this 37-mile (60 km) loop, starting in the pretty little seaport of La Flotte, known for its food market. Scarcely do you get any pace up before you arrive at the UNESCO World Heritage–listed fortified seaport of Saint-Martin-de-Ré. The town's fortifications were laid out in 1681 by Sébastien Le Prestre de Vauban, one of history's greatest military engineers, to help secure the coast and nearby La Rochelle.

From Saint-Martin-de-Ré, the route follows a beautiful stretch of coast, past oyster beds and the shimmering fields of the island's famous sea salt industry. For such a small island, Île de Ré offers a surprising diversity of landscapes, including woodlands, vineyards, marshes, poppy fields, and a succession of charming villages.

At the island's westernmost tip, you come to the 200-foot-tall (61 m) Lighthouse of the Whales, built in 1854. Climb to the top for a sweeping panorama of the island. This is your turnaround point. Loop back to La Flotte via La Couarde-sur-Mer. From Le Bois-Plage-en-Ré, another beach town, pedal across the island—it's only a couple of miles wide—back to where you began.

CYCLING THROUGH HISTORY

Saint-Martin-de-Ré, located only two miles (3.2 km) away from La Flotte, is home to the Vauban citadel, which held convicts bound for penal colonies in French Guiana and New Caledonia. Book a tour via the local tourism office.

OPPOSITE: The red-tipped Lighthouse of Saint-Martin-de-Ré in Charente-Maritime

BERLIN WALL TRAIL

Follow the route of the infamous wall that once divided East from West, from the Brandenburg Gate to the Bridge of Spies.

DISTANCE: **100 miles (161 km)**   SURFACE: **Mixed; mostly paved**   LENGTH OF TRIP: **2 to 4 days**
WHEN TO GO: **Spring through autumn**   DIFFICULTY: **Easy**

A fascinating ride takes you through Berlin and its surrounding countryside along the perimeter of the infamous Berlin Wall, the barrier that divided East from West for nearly 30 years and came to be one of the most potent symbols of the Cold War.

Start at the Berlin Wall Memorial, which runs along both sides of Bernauer Strasse, once part of the border strip between East and West Berlin. As well as the official memorial, there is a permanent exhibition on the history and building of the wall, with historical radio broadcasts and stories of tunnels dug from one side to the other, and one of the original watchtowers from which guards monitored this stretch of the border.

The path zigzags through the city, just as the wall once did, alternately passing famous landmarks such the Reichstag building, Brandenburg Gate, and Checkpoint Charlie and cutting through ordinary neighborhoods and industrial areas. It is a genuine slice of Berlin.

Although it is called the Berlin Wall Trail, surprisingly little of the actual wall remains. After the Iron Curtain came down in 1989, there were strong feelings, particularly among East Germans, that the "Wall of Shame" ought to be obliterated and the whole sorry episode forgotten. It was West Berliners who sought to preserve the memory of it, with twin lines of cobbles marking the route where the wall once stood. The longest remaining stretch—4,318 feet (1,316 m) of it—is found along the banks of the River Spree near Muhlenstrasse. Known as the East Side Gallery, it is emblazoned with colorful murals painted

OPPOSITE: Cyclists pass a portion of the East Side Gallery in East Berlin.

PAGES 300-301: Historic photographs are on display along the Berlin Wall Trail at Bernauer Strasse.

Bernauer Straße

Strümpfe

by 118 artists from 21 countries, making it also the world's longest open-air art gallery.

Two-thirds of the path lies outside the city, running through forests and meadows where the wall wasn't so much a wall as a barbed-wire fence surrounded by exposed terrain once known as the "death zone," overlain with booby traps and trip wires and monitored by guards.

Near Potsdam, southwest of the city, you'll cross Glienicke Bridge, known as the Bridge of Spies, where the U.S. and Soviet governments exchanged captured spies during the Cold War—most famously in 1962 when the United States swapped Soviet spy Rudolf Abel for American spy-plane pilot Francis Gary Powers.

For all its chilling Cold War history, a ride along the Berlin Wall is far from gloomy. The former death zone is now a pleasant forest path, and the city has flourished into one of Europe's most vibrant capitals. Indeed, the Berlin Wall Trail would be a delightful bicycle ride even without the history. Scenic, flat, well signposted, and nearly traffic free, it is a wonderful way to explore the area and easy to do in stages.

CYCLING THROUGH HISTORY

Well over 100,000 attempts were made to escape East Germany between 1961 and 1989. While the exact number of those who tried to escape over the Berlin Wall is unknown, at least 140 died in their attempts. Further information on the history of the wall, as well as a travel guide for following its route, can be had on the free Berlin Wall app.

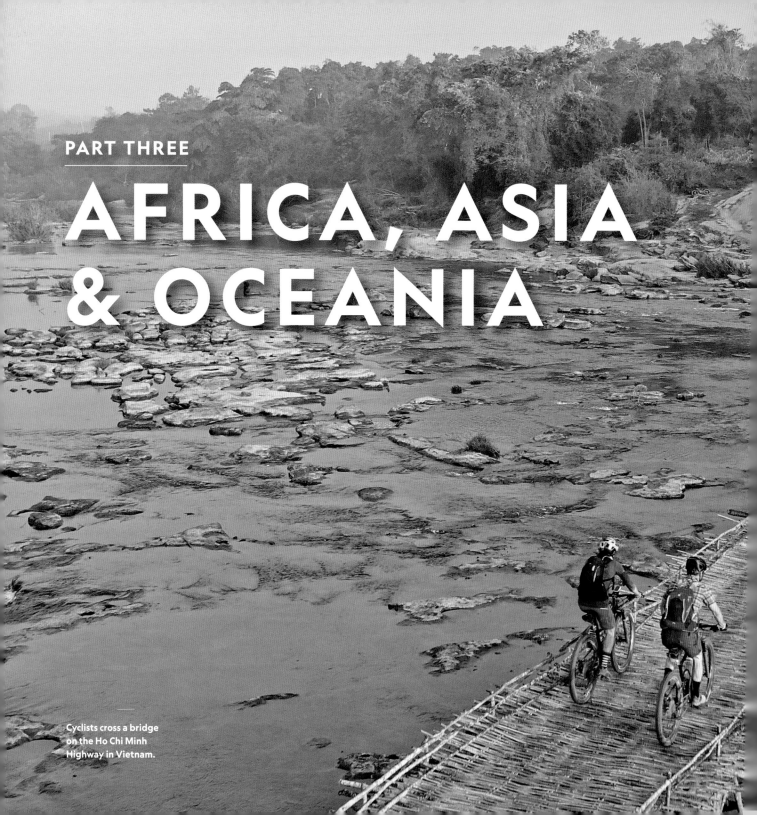

PART THREE

AFRICA, ASIA & OCEANIA

Cyclists cross a bridge
on the Ho Chi Minh
Highway in Vietnam.

SWARTBERG PASS

Ride over one of the world's most spectacular mountain passes in South Africa's hauntingly remote Karoo region—and take a side trip into "the Hell."

DISTANCE: **85 miles (137 km)**   SURFACE: **Mixed; paved, gravel**   LENGTH OF TRIP: **1 to 2 days**
WHEN TO GO: **Spring or autumn**   DIFFICULTY: **Challenging**

Cycling South Africa's World Heritage–listed Swartberg Pass—with its craggy black-rock cliff faces, sweeping views over the vast arid region known as the Karoo, and switchbacks that fly over the historic 19th-century track's 5,193-foot (1,583 m) pass—is regarded as one of the world's great bucket-list rides. It can be made even more memorable with an out-and-back side trip through a remote valley known as Die Hel (the Hell) to the lonely farmstead of Gamkaskloof.

This is a ride for gravel or mountain bikes. The journey starts at Prince Albert, a small, pretty, whitewashed town surrounded by vineyards and olive groves that's about a five-hour drive from Cape Town. Head south on a paved road and then onto the narrow gravel track that climbs into the mountains and over the pass. It was built during the 1880s by Thomas Charles Bain, one of South Africa's great roadbuilding engineers, using convict labor and dry stone retaining walls to support the road as it zigzags its precarious way up the steep flanks of the mountain.

Both sides of Swartberg Pass are spectacular, but the approach from the Prince Albert side is especially so, with increasingly dramatic views with every rising turn. Just before you reach the top of the pass, on the right, is the rough gravel track that descends into one of the most isolated valleys in South Africa.

Until the early 1960s there was no road into this hidden valley. The road was built to access the extremely remote farming community at Gamkaskloof

OPPOSITE: A dusty road weaves between craggy mountains in the Swartberg Pass.

PAGES 306-307: The gravelly switchbacks of Swartberg Pass lead riders through some of the most isolated regions of South Africa.

that, since its settlement in 1830, had largely been cut off from the outside world. The road into Gamkaskloof turned out to be the road out of it as well, with the young quickly departing for opportunities elsewhere. The last farmer left Gamkaskloof in 1991. Today accommodation is available in the restored cottages for those who make it that far and want to stay.

It's a challenging ride up the valley, along a winding, hilly gravel track that makes 201 bends in the 17 miles (27 km) from near the top of Swartberg Pass. The scenery is stunning, which will make you wonder how this wild, beautiful valley could ever have been nicknamed Die Hel. The exact origins of the name are obscure, but the popular story has it that a government minister had to make the arduous journey into Gamkaskloof in the 1940s and didn't relish the experience.

The ride out of Die Hel is the same as the ride in, following the same winding gravel track back up to near the summit of Swartberg Pass. Once you rejoin the old road, you crest the pass and start the long and beautiful descent toward Oudtshoorn and the finish of one of South Africa's greatest bike rides.

CYCLING THROUGH HISTORY

Back in Victorian and Edwardian days, when feathers were mainstays on ladies' hats, the ostrich-farming town of Oudtshoorn was the place to make your fortune. The glory days ended around 1914 when open-topped motorcars curbed demand for elaborate feathered hats.

CONGO-NILE TRAIL

Pedal the shores of one of Africa's Great Lakes through a landscape of jungle-clad mountains and tea plantations.

DISTANCE: **141 miles (227 km)**   SURFACE: **Mixed**   LENGTH OF TRIP: **5 days**
WHEN TO GO: **June through September (dry season)**   DIFFICULTY: **Moderate to challenging**

R wanda is one of the world's great undiscovered cycle-touring destinations, offering a superb introduction to Africa in one of the continent's safest, friendliest, and most stable countries—and one with a thriving local cycling culture to boot.

And there's no better way to explore Rwanda than along the Congo-Nile Trail. Developed in 2011 for use by hikers and cyclists, it follows the shores of Lake Kivu, one of the African Great Lakes, and passes through a cavalcade of lush mountainous landscapes, rainforests, and terraced tea, coffee, and banana plantations, with ample guesthouses and campsites along the way. It is by no means an easy ride—a total of more than 19,000 feet (5,790 m) of climbing is involved, with the trail reaching a high point of 8,200 feet (2,499 m), but the scenery, bright tropical birds , butterflies, and other wildlife, flowers, and sense of adventure more than repay the effort.

Most people start the journey at the northern end of the trail in Gisenyi, a large provincial town readily accessible by bus from Rwanda's capital, Kigali. It's about a four-hour journey, and if you're bringing your own bike, you'll need to pay for a seat for it as well; it's not expensive.

Most of the route south of Gisenyi is along jungle tracks and dirt roads, although in recent years the southernmost stretch of the trail into Kamembe

OPPOSITE: The trail curves along the water near Karongi in Rwanda.

PAGES 310-11: Grab a bite in beautiful Rubavu, a resort town on the shores of Rwanda's Lake Kivu.

has been paved—an improvement for motorists but one that has divided cyclists, with some preferring the old rough-and-ready dirt track and others welcoming a chance to ride on smooth tarmac. For hikers and those cyclists keen on keeping off the pavement, alternate paths—some of them challenging singletrack—have been cobbled together.

The first day or so along the trail is the easiest and takes you through some of the loveliest scenery along the entire route, following well-made jungle tracks that skirt the edge of the lake and through a string of picturesque fishing villages. The going gets tougher as you go farther south, with some steep climbs into the tea-growing highlands and Nyungwe rainforest. The Congo-Nile Trail, by the way, is so named because it follows the mountainous divide between the watershed of these two great rivers, not because the trail goes near the rivers themselves.

The stretch of road through Nyungwe National

ALTERNATE ROUTE

Rwanda is an increasingly prominent player in professional road-racing circles, with the Tour of Rwanda attracting pros from around the world and the UCI Road World Championships to be hosted here in 2025. There's also the new Race Around Rwanda, a 625-mile (1,006 km) endurance event held in February. It's a tough course around the perimeter of the nation, with 40 percent on gravel and the rest on smooth tarmac. Riders have to be self-supporting and complete the ride in just under six days (139 hours).

Park is beautiful but rough and primitive, and in the rain it can be very muddy—a good reason to do this trek during the dry season. Rwanda's climate is relatively mild, temperature-wise, for tropical Africa, but its rainy seasons are legendary. If you are not up for the adventure of the Nyungwe rainforest's rough tracks, an easier paved alternative exists, although by taking it you'll miss some wonderful opportunities for wildlife-spotting, including Rwanda's 13 species of primates.

The final 30 miles (48 km) of the trail into Kamembe are mainly along smooth tarmac. At Kamembe you can either catch a bus to Kigali or, if you'd like to see more of the lake, take a nine-hour boat journey back to your starting point at Gisenyi.

CAPE OF GOOD HOPE

Explore the unique fynbos ecosystem of the World Heritage–listed Cape Point Nature Reserve.

DISTANCE: **Up to 37 miles (60 km)**   SURFACE: **Paved**   LENGTH OF TRIP: **1 day**
WHEN TO GO: **March through May or September through November**   DIFFICULTY: **Easy**

W hen Portuguese explorer Bartolomeu Dias rounded the southernmost tip of Africa in 1488, he named the point of land he saw the Cape of Storms. Even on the sunniest day there is often a stiff breeze. It was his king who came up with the more optimistic name of Cape of Good Hope, reflecting his ambitions for the new seaborne spice route around Africa to India.

More than 500 years—and no small number of shipwrecks—later, the Cape of Good Hope is a UNESCO World Heritage–listed landmark and a pleasant place to explore on two wheels. Located some 37 miles (60 km) south of Cape Town, the 19,000-acre (7,689 ha) Cape Point Nature Reserve offers miles of riding along paved road, taking in beautiful beaches, dramatic cliffs, and rolling expanses of fynbos, a uniquely South African heathland that is the smallest, richest, and most diverse of Earth's six distinct floral kingdoms.

The ride starts at the entrance to Cape Point Nature Reserve and follows the park road down the peninsula to the tip of the cape, with possibilities for side trips to pretty beaches and dramatic viewpoints branching off on both sides of the road. Fifteen miles (24 km) will bring you to the turnoff for the Cape of Good Hope, while riding for another three miles (4.8 km) will take you to Cape Point, with its historic lighthouse and resident baboon population.

OPPOSITE: **Riders pause along the Cape Peninsula in Cape Town.**

QINGHAI LAKE

Adventure on the roof of the world! Pedal around a vast inland sea teeming with birdlife on the high Tibetan Plateau.

DISTANCE: **241 miles (388 km)**   SURFACE: **Paved**   LENGTH OF TRIP: **4 days**
WHEN TO GO: **May through October**   DIFFICULTY: **Moderate**

Sitting high on the windswept grasslands of the Tibetan Plateau at nearly 11,000 feet (3,350 m), Qinghai Lake is China's largest inland body of water, a vast salt lake spreading over some 1,653 square miles (4,281 sq km) that is home to more than half a million migratory birds. Since 2002 the lake has also been a focal point for one of Asia's top professional bike races, the Tour of Qinghai Lake, a 10-day stage race held each July around the same time as the Tour de France.

While the pros ride a tough 924-mile (1,487 km) circuit through Qinghai Province, the 223-mile (359 km) loop around Qinghai Lake itself has become a honeypot for touring cyclists looking for adventure. The loop starts at the town of Xihaizhen, about 100 miles (161 km) from the provincial capital Xining. Most riders travel clockwise, in keeping with Tibetan beliefs, and have the lake on their right as they make their way around. Roads are good, and the route is generally flat, although the high altitude can make itself felt, as can the nippy temperatures early in the mornings, even during summer.

The scenery is haunting in its beauty and desolation: sweeping expanses of Tibetan grasslands and dazzling yellow fields of canola in midsummer, with towering mountain ranges in the distance and the vivid lapis blue waters of the lake (its name literally means "blue lake"). There are plenty of places to rent bicycles in Xihaizhen, and there's no shortage of food options and accommodation around the lake. May and June are good months to come if you want to see the birdlife, while the canola fields are spectacular in July and August.

OPPOSITE: **A rainbow-hued line of riders is reflected in the still waters of the lake during the Tour of Qinghai Lake race in 2022.**

4 RIVERS PATH

Spoil yourself on one of the world's most extravagant bicycle paths—complete with pagoda-like shelters for campers and colored lights illuminating the tunnels.

DISTANCE: **393 miles (632 km)**   SURFACE: **Mixed**   LENGTH OF TRIP: **5 to 7 days**
WHEN TO GO: **Spring**   DIFFICULTY: **Easy to moderate**

How's this for stylish adventure? Pedal the length of one of Asia's prettiest, safest, most cycling-friendly nations on a fabulously well-thought-out bicycle path that's nearly level and traffic free the entire way—and then receive a medal from the government for completing the journey. Small wonder that South Korea's 4 Rivers Path has become a must-do bucket-list ride for touring cyclists in the know.

Although South Korea is better known internationally for K-pop than cycling, in recent years its government has been pouring money into cycling infrastructure, and the 4 Rivers Path, completed in 2015, is the showpiece. Stretching between Incheon in the north and the port city of Busan along the southeast coast, it is a superb way to explore South Korea and offers novice cycle tourers a wonderful introduction to the world of long-haul touring—if also a pleasantly misleading one, since you won't find this level of catering and trailside amenities very many other places. There's no shortage of convenience stores, guesthouses, restaurants, toilet facilities, and elegant gazebo-like structures for camping all located right on the trail. There's even a bicycle museum at Sangju, near the southern end of the trail. And if you go during the spring, you can enjoy the cherry blossoms, which add to the parklike feel of riding this trail.

As its name implies, the path follows four of South Korea's major rivers—the Han, Nakdong, Geum, and Yeongsan—as it wends its way through the heart of the country. The path is generally flat or rolling, through forests and across

OPPOSITE: **The Yeongsan bike path, part of the 4 Rivers Path, in Gwangju**

PAGES 320-21: **A cyclist takes photos of the Seoul skyline beside the Han River.**

rice paddies, but about halfway along the route the trail climbs up and over a mountain pass at Ihwaryeong, which is only 1,640 feet (500 m) but, after so many miles of flat riding, seems higher. From there, the route descends to join the Nakdong River, which it follows for the rest of the ride into Busan.

The engineering of the bicycle path is as spectacular as the scenery. Where possible in some of the hillier stretches, the designers went to the trouble and expense of boring tunnels through the hillsides—yes, just for a bicycle path. And they're not dark and dingy tunnels either, but colorfully lit. And for a couple of miles along an otherwise inaccessible stretch of the left bank of the Nakdong on the approach to Busan, the path runs along a specially built pierlike structure overhanging the river.

Most thru-riders begin their journeys in Incheon. Before you start, pick up your trail passport so you can accumulate the stamps along the

ALTERNATE ROUTE

South Korea's network of cycle paths extends to more than just the showpiece route between Incheon and Busan. Two of the country's lesser known gems in the 4 Rivers network are the 91-mile (146 km) ride along the Geum River, between Daejeon and Gunsan, and the 83-mile (134 km) ride along the Yeongsan River in the southwest. The Geum River ride takes in the ancient mountain fortresses and tombs of Korea's Baekje dynasty, while the Yeongsan River route offers a fascinating glimpse into a rural Korea often missed by tourists.

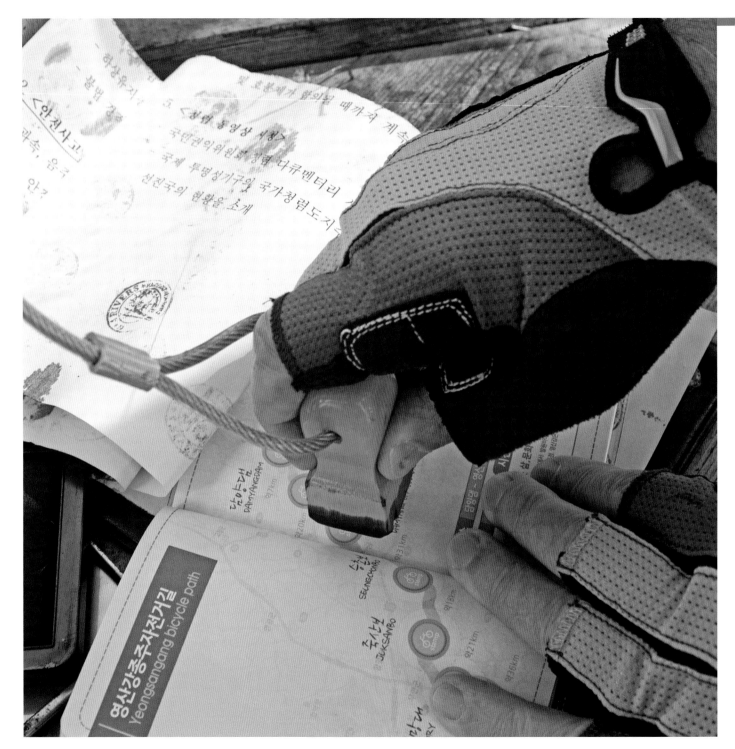

ABOVE: A statue speaks to the friendly atmosphere along the traffic-free Yeongsan River path.

OPPOSITE: Don't forget to get your 4 Rivers Path passport stamped at the checkpoint booths along the trail.

way to earn your medal. Blank passports are available at certification centers at both ends of the trail. Fill them in with stamps as you go, pausing at the red checkpoint booths you'll come to along the way to record your progress. Collect all the stamps and earn a medal from the tourist information office at the end of your ride.

Once clear of the glass-and-steel sprawl of Incheon and Seoul, you'll be in quiet countryside, following scenic rivers through rural small-town South Korea for most of the journey. English is not widely spoken, but smiles are plentiful and translate well. Life on the road couldn't be more serene or gently paced—or better catered to. And if at the end of your ride you feel like a sleek reintroduction to the faster-paced world of the 21st century, just catch the KTX bullet train from Busan back to Seoul at 190 miles an hour (306 km/h).

SHIMANAMI KAIDO

Island-hop across Japan's beautiful Seto Inland Sea
on an exquisite, purpose-built cycleway.

DISTANCE: **43 miles (69 km)**   SURFACE: **Paved**   LENGTH OF TRIP: **1 to 2 days**
WHEN TO GO: **Summer through autumn**   DIFFICULTY: **Easy**

Using a network of bridges and six islands as stepping stones, the Shimanami Kaido bicycle path crosses the Mediterranean-like Seto Inland Sea in western Japan, connecting Onomichi near Hiroshima with the town of Imabari on the opposite shore.

Built in 1999, the traffic-free bicycle path follows a leisurely course and is six miles (9.6 km) longer than the vehicular version—to spare cyclists the steep inclines on the high-arching bridges.

It's a stunning ride, offering magnificent sea views and opportunities to explore each of the six stepping-stone islands it touches on its way across the sea. The islands themselves—Mukaishima, Innoshima, Ikuchijima, Omishima, Hakatajima, and Oshima—are quietly rural, known for their orange groves, beautiful shrines, gardens, and local gelato.

Since this is a point-to-point ride, you can start at either end, although most riders choose to begin at Onomichi because of the excellent transport links to nearby Hiroshima. Navigation is easy; just follow the painted blue line that marks the path. It is not a demanding ride, with most of the climbing being on the ramps for the bridges. The steepest gradients you'll come across are on the Kurushima-Kaikyo Bridge and on the hilly island of Oshima, both of which are about 200 feet (60 m) above sea level.

OPPOSITE: A cyclist circles the sky on the Kurushima-Kaikyo Bridge, the world's longest suspension bridge.

ANCIENT ANGKOR

Escape the crowds and explore the ruins of the sprawling ninth-century Khmer capital on a network of quiet, shady paths that are perfect for cycling.

DISTANCE: **12 miles (19 km)**　SURFACE: **Mixed**　LENGTH OF TRIP: **3 days**
WHEN TO GO: **November through February**　DIFFICULTY: **Easy**

Witnessing the sunrise over Angkor Wat is one of those classic bucket-list travel aspirations. Every morning at dawn, especially during the peak-season winter months, hundreds of tourists can be seen lining up with cameras at the ready, waiting for the sun's first rays to illuminate the flanks of this magnificent 12th-century temple.

What's often overlooked in all the glamour surrounding Angkor Wat itself is that it is but one of literally scores of ancient temples and crumbling ruins in a sprawling archaeological site that's spread out over 150 square miles (390 sq km). Most visitors see only the headline attraction and a couple of nearby shrines. To explore this astonishing World Heritage site fully and escape the crowds, you need to break free of the herd, and there's no better way to do that than on a bicycle.

It's easily done. Bicycle rentals are cheap and plentiful in Siem Reap, the town nearest to the ancient city of Angkor, and the four-mile (6.4 km) ride out to the site—known as the Angkor Archaeological Park—is on a flat road with a bicycle path running along it. By purchasing a three-day pass from the visitors center, or a seven-day one if you're especially keen, you'll have plenty of time to explore and, with a bicycle, the flexibility and independence to do it justice.

There is far more to see here than just Angkor Wat. This is one of the world's largest archaeological sites, comprising more than 70 temples built

OPPOSITE: **A stone gate of Angkor Thom in Cambodia**

PAGES 328-29: **A group of cyclists pass Bayon Temple in the Angkor Archaeological Park.**

between the ninth and 12th centuries, together with a network of canals, dikes, reservoirs, and water features. Among the other popular sites are the iconic Bayon temple, with its colossal stone faces; the temple Ta Prohm, with its intriguing stonework in the grip of the roots of huge trees, as featured in the 2001 film *Lara Croft: Tomb Raider* with Angelina Jolie; and the walled city of Angkor Thom. But there are dozens of smaller, lesser known temples, many of which you can have virtually to yourself.

Finding your way around is easy, and over three days you can see much of the site, creating your own loops and circuits. Maps of the park are available, and the temples themselves are not that far apart—seldom more than a 15-minute ride between them—while the roads and paths on which you ride are flat, usually quiet, and, since much of the park is forested, often in shade.

PHOTO OP

The 10th-century ruined temple at Phnom Bok is among the oldest and least visited sites in the vast Angkor complex, and yet it is also one of the most beautiful and evocative. Located about 13 miles (21 km) northeast of Siem Reap, on good sealed roads, the temple sits atop a 700-foot-high (213 m) hill and is accessible by climbing more than 600 steps—hard work, but the peaceful setting, the ruin itself, and the distant views from the hilltop more than repay the effort.

SUN MOON LAKE

Pedal though a painterly landscape of mists, floating gardens, and temples along this loop around Asia's most beautiful alpine lake.

DISTANCE: **19 miles (30 km)**   SURFACE: **Mixed**   LENGTH OF TRIP: **1 day**
WHEN TO GO: **Spring or autumn**   DIFFICULTY: **Moderate**

Sun Moon Lake is one of the world's most beautiful alpine lakes, nestled in the mountains in central Taiwan. Riding the bicycle path that loops around it is a magical experience, like pedaling through a succession of fine old watercolors.

It's a hilly ride in places, as the foothills come right up to the edge of the lake. But the views repay the effort, with panoramas of lush mountains and reflections off Sun Moon Lake, whose jewel-like waters, from turquoise to a luminous sapphire blue, have inspired poets for centuries. The lake gets its curious name from its shape. Divided by an island in its center, the eastern half resembles the sun, while the western half resembles a crescent moon.

Start your ride at Shuishe, the main town along the lake. Bicycles are available to rent here if you haven't brought your own. As you make your way around the lake, through miles of shady bamboo forests, over hills, and along wooden cycleways that run, pierlike, over the water, you'll also pass four beautiful temples—among them Wenwu, guarded by the largest stone lions in Asia and whose terrace offers spectacular views over the lake, and the 150-foot-high (46 m) Ci'en Pagoda, erected by Taiwan's former leader Chiang Kai-shek in honor of his mother. If you're here during the spring, this is also a good place to see the area's famous black-winged fireflies emerge in the evening.

TOP TIP: Start riding Sun Moon Lake in the cool of early morning, when you'll have the path largely to yourself and the lake and mountains are bathed in gossamer mists.

OPPOSITE: **The stunning Sun Moon Lake in Taiwan**

MAE HONG SON LOOP

With steep climbs and corkscrew descents, this route through the cloud forest mountains of northern Thailand is unforgettable—and not for the faint of heart.

DISTANCE: **410 miles (660 km)**   SURFACE: **Paved**   LENGTH OF TRIP: **7 to 10 days**
WHEN TO GO: **November through February (dry season)**   DIFFICULTY: **Challenging**

A spectacular ride through mist-shrouded mountains, the Mae Hong Son Loop is not exactly the route you want to pick if you're making your first foray into cycle touring. On narrow, winding roads with more than 4,000 curves involving a total of more than 43,000 feet (13,105 m) of climbing and gradients up to 30 percent, it is no place for beginners. But if you're up for the challenge, doing the Mae Hong Son circuit is an adventure of a lifetime.

The ride starts in Chiang Mai. The first 20 miles (32 km) or so are on a flat and fairly busy road, but the traffic and the easy pedaling fall away once you turn off the main highway toward Pai. The road narrows, and wide expanses of rice paddies give way to some serious climbing as you head into the mountains of rural Thailand. Gradients exceed 10 percent, and for long stretches the road writhes its way through the rainforest to nearly 4,600 feet (1,400 m), followed by an exhilarating 3,000-foot (914 m) corkscrew of a descent into Pai.

This popular town on the backpacker circuit is a good place to spend your first night on the road. Because of its popularity, plenty of accommodations and great street food are on offer. Eat heartily. Another steep and winding climb awaits the next morning, the road rising through the mists to nearly

OPPOSITE: **A flight of stairs leads to the sacred pilgrimage site of Wat Phra That Doi Suthep in Chiang Mai.**

PAGES 334-35: **Sunset at Doi Inthanon National Park in Chiang Mai**

5,000 feet (1,525 m) before making another plunging descent, this time into Soppong and a series of short, punchy climbs as you make your way to Mae Hong Son.

Mae Hong Son is quieter than Pai, with a laid-back vibe that marks a bit of a transition in the ride. From here you get a breather for a couple of days, with the next 100 miles (161 km) or so being relatively easy, rolling through pleasantly shady forests on good roads and, in season, past fields of sunflowers—a Tour de France touch—as you make your way to Mae Sariang.

Mae Sariang is another relaxed town on the banks of a scenic river and a nice place to lay over for a day, because after this you're back to climbing into the mists and rainforests on these winding and narrow mountain roads, making plunging descents, and pedaling

PHOTO OP

Doi Inthanon is one of Thailand's most popular national parks, 186 square miles (482 sq km) of cloud forest wilderness nestled in a pocket of mountains known as the Roof of Thailand, part of the Himalaya. The park is famed for its waterfalls, bird-watching, and Siamese sakura (cherry blossom) flowers. Sunrise from the 8,415-foot (2,565 m) summit of the park's namesake mountain, Doi Inthanon, is one of the park's biggest draws. Also popular is the Kew Mae Pan Nature Trail, a circular two-mile (3.2 km) hiking path that offers spectacular panoramic views.

ABOVE: A pair of bikers ascend to the summit of Doi Inthanon with the misty mountains in the background.

OPPOSITE: A colorful sign-post in Pai, northern Thailand

along ridgelines with views over the valleys. Eighty miles (129 km) brings you to Mae Chaem and the start of a grade that ranks with some of the classic alpine ascents—more than 10 miles (16 km) at an average gradient of 7 percent. At the top of the climb, amid the cloud forests, you have an option to turn off the road and take a six-mile (9.6 km) side trip to the summit of Doi Inthanon, Thailand's highest mountain, at 8,481 feet (2,585 m). It's a tough haul pedaling up to the summit but worth it. The views are magnificent, and from here it's all downhill—a breezy 25-mile (40 km) descent back to the main road and your return to Chiang Mai.

HO CHI MINH HIGHWAY

This legendary road is one of Asia's great long-haul cycling adventures, but the section that runs through the mountainous region along the Laotian border is truly special.

DISTANCE: **137 miles (220 km)**   SURFACE: **Paved**   LENGTH OF TRIP: **3 days**
WHEN TO GO: **November through March**   DIFFICULTY: **Challenging**

Vietnam's Ho Chi Minh Highway is one of Southeast Asia's most beloved long-haul bicycle rides, meandering more than 1,000 miles (1,610 km) through jungle-clad mountains and across rice paddies from Ho Chi Minh City in the south to the country's capital city, Hanoi, in the north. For much of its length it approximates the route of the famed Ho Chi Minh Trail, the network of secret paths along which the Vietcong transported weapons and troops during the Vietnam War.

It's a prettier, much more rural, and much less trafficked option than Vietnam's coastal Highway 1, which connects the same two cities. But for those who don't have the time for a 1,000-mile (1,610 km) cycling odyssey, the spectacular 137-mile (220 km) stretch in the middle, through the mountains between Khe Sanh and Phong Nha, is the highlight of the ride and worthy of a listing on its own.

This is the wildest, most beautiful and remote section of the highway, running through the mountains along the Laotian border. Once you leave Khe Sanh behind, heading north, you're pretty much on your own. There are few villages along this stretch of the highway, just miles of lush tropical rainforest, tumbling rivers, waterfalls, and stunning mountain views at every bend. Long Son, a picturesque hamlet about halfway between Khe Sanh and

OPPOSITE: Bike through a lush jungle on the remote Ho Chi Minh Highway.

PAGES 340-41: Verdant mountain views abound on the Ho Chi Minh Highway.

Phong Nha, has accommodation and shops where you can buy meals and supplies.

Incredibly, the scenery gets only more spectacular as you pedal farther north and into Phong Nha-Ke Bang National Park. The limestone karst landscape here has eroded over millions of years into hundreds of eerie cones, pillars, and pinnacles, all clad in dense jungle. It's like pedaling through a lost world. Indeed, until recently this little-known landscape harbored a remarkable secret: Son Doong, the world's largest cave by volume at more than 50 million cubic yards (38 million cubic m), was surveyed by an expedition in 2009. It's one of a number of vast caves in the region, some of which are open to the public.

After so many miles of remote mountain roads, arriving at Phong Nha is a bit of a shock. It's a bustling place, popular with backpackers who've come to see the caves in the nearby national park. If you're looking for accommodation, press on a couple of miles north of the town center, where you can find some rural homestays with lovely views over the remarkable landscapes through which you've just ridden.

KNOW BEFORE YOU GO

Go a little farther off the beaten track while you're in the Phong Nha area and explore the lovely Bong Lai Valley, an unspoiled pocket of farmland, rice paddies, dirt roads, and villages. All you need are a map and a bicycle (a gravel bike is best, given the unpaved roads and tracks). Farm stays are available if you want to spend a little more time in this hidden gem of old Vietnam.

MANALI-LEH HIGHWAY

Follow a legendary trade route over the 17,582-foot (5,359 m) Tanglang Pass to the capital of the ancient mountain kingdom of Ladakh.

DISTANCE: **294 miles (473 km)**   SURFACE: **Mixed**   LENGTH OF TRIP: **10 to 12 days**
WHEN TO GO: **June through September**   DIFFICULTY: **Extreme**

India's Manali-Leh Highway is a bucket-list legend among globe-trotting cyclists, offering romance, adventure, and scenery that literally takes your breath away, with the highway climbing to more than 17,000 feet (5,180 m) on its way to Leh, the historic capital and largest city of Ladakh, in the mountains.

The ride starts at Manali, about a 12-hour bus ride from Delhi. Manali is a popular base for trekking, mountaineering, and rafting—and at 6,700 feet (2,042 m) is a good place to linger for a day or two to acclimatize before tackling the Manali-Leh Highway. The road ahead of you reaches some serious elevation, crosses five major mountain passes, and averages more than 13,000 feet (3,960 m). Also, Manali is a good place to double-check your bike, tools, spares, and equipment list, because while there are villages and guesthouses along the way to pick up food or spend the night, if you suddenly find that you're missing an important bit of gear, you'll be stuck.

Setting out from Manali, the road heads north and rears steeply upward, climbing to more than 11,000 feet (3,350 m) within the first 20 miles (32 km). Lofty though this may seem, it's merely your initial cruising altitude, with five towering mountain passes coming up. The first of these is Rohtang, at 13,050 feet (3,978 m), which you'll reach on your second or third day on the road,

OPPOSITE: **The misty Rohtang Pass in the Indian Himalaya**

PAGES 344-45: **Cyclists find some shade amid the cliffs as they near the village of Pang.**

depending on what kind of a start you make out of Manali and how heavy the traffic is along the highway. It can be quite hectic, but happily enough, after Rohtang Pass the road is vastly quieter.

After a breezy descent down Rohtang Pass, follow the Chandra River into Sissu, where the road once again begins to climb. It winds its way ever upward into the Himalaya over the next few days. Along the way, the road takes you through villages such as Zingzingbar (at 14,009 feet/ 4,270 meters), Pang (15,091 feet/4,600 meters), and Debring (15,862 feet/4,835 meters). In between them it crosses a series of even higher-altitude mountain passes before culminating in the 17,582-foot (5,359 m) Tanglang Pass, the highest point along the route, with its Buddhist monument and prayer flags and spectacular views of the Zanskar and Ladakh mountain ranges.

From Tanglang Pass the road winds its way down to Upshi, losing more than a mile in elevation, and on down through fertile valleys another 30 miles (48 km) or so to the end of your journey at Leh.

ALTERNATE ROUTE

If for some reason the dizzying elevation of Tanglang Pass (17,582 feet/5,359 meters) isn't enough of a challenge, you can always press on another 25 miles (40 km) from Leh up the flanks of 18,380-foot (5,602 m) Khardung Pass, on the old road to the Nubra Valley. If you'd like to sample the razor-thin air but don't fancy the uphill climb, local outfitters in Leh can drive you to the top and let you enjoy the exhilarating descent.

PAMIR HIGHWAY

Follow the old Silk Road across the sweeping vastness of high Central Asia.

DISTANCE: **777 miles (1,250 km)**   SURFACE: **Mainly paved**   LENGTH OF TRIP: **3 to 4 weeks**
WHEN TO GO: **August through September**   DIFFICULTY: **Challenging**

The Pamir Highway approximates the route of the legendary Silk Road through high Central Asia and makes for an all-time classic long-haul cycling expedition. It is not a journey to be undertaken lightly: The regions it traverses are extremely remote; the road is often rough, unpaved, and climbs to more than 15,000 feet (4,570 m); and riders have to be reasonably self-reliant. But it is nevertheless a doable adventure for anyone with good fitness and a sturdy gravel bike.

Starting in Dushanbe, Tajikistan's capital city, and traveling east is the easiest option. Eastbound travelers are more likely to have the wind at their backs rather than have to fight headwinds. Heading east also allows you to put off the highest pass, Ak-Baital, until later in the journey when you're better acclimated. Late summer is the best time to go. The valleys can be lovely in spring, but snow on the high passes can make it impossible to get through. September is an especially pleasant time—it's harvest season, so local produce along the way is plentiful, and the autumn colors can be beautiful.

Dushanbe is a good place to give your bicycle a final check, as there are no bicycle shops along the route. Stock up on provisions, as resupply points are few and far between. The highway—its official name is the much less romantic M41—was paved by the Soviets in the 1930s and hasn't had a lot of maintenance since, but it has been battered by avalanches, landslides, earthquakes, and decades of harsh weathering.

While the road may be badly potholed, the scenery through which it runs is magnificent, the landscape opening up wide, its vastness and timelessness

OPPOSITE: Mountains tower in the distance as cyclists near the border between Tajikistan and Kyrgyzstan.

PAGES 348-49: The final leg of the Pamir Highway extends from the mountains and on to the Kyrgyzstan border.

a pleasant reminder that you're traveling a centuries-old trade route. A few days out of Dushanbe, you come to your first mountain. At just over 10,000 feet (3,050 m), it is a mere taste of the dizzying heights to come.

Here you are literally a stone's throw from Afghanistan. The Panj River, which flows past Kalaikhum, forms this stretch of the Tajik-Afghan border. For the next few days you follow the river through the towns of Rushan—especially pretty in autumn—and Khorog, where the road makes a sharp northerly turn toward the Pamir Plateau. The road climbs to the crest of Koi Tezek Pass, at 14,015 feet (4,272 m). It's desolate up here, and even in summer the nights are cold, but the solitude is haunting and the starry nights spectacular. The literal high point of the journey is Ak-Baital Pass, at 15,272 feet (4,655 m). A swooping descent brings you to the town of Karakol and its sprawling mountain lake, and beyond that the Kyrgyzstan border. From there, a little over 100 miles (161 km) will bring you to Osh.

CYCLING THROUGH HISTORY

The Silk Road—or more accurately, Silk Routes—was a network of ancient trade routes between the East and West dating back to around 140 B.C., when China's Han dynasty opened its doors to trade with the West. Stretching more than 4,000 miles (6,435 km) from China to Constantinople and Damascus, with branch lines into India, it was the major conduit for silks, spices, and ideas until the 15th century. The Pamir Highway approximates one of the original Silk Routes.

YAS MARINA CIRCUIT

Go for a spin around one of the world's fastest Formula 1 circuits.

DISTANCE: **3 miles (5 km)**   SURFACE: **Paved**   LENGTH OF TRIP: **I day**
WHEN TO GO: **Year-round**   DIFFICULTY: **Easy**

Ever dreamed of taking your bicycle for a spin around one of the world's great F1 tracks? You can do precisely that at Abu Dhabi's Yas Marina Circuit on weekday evenings and mornings, when the $800 million facility is thrown open to walkers, runners, and cyclists.

It's part of a community health and fitness initiative designed to get people moving and active. With summer daytime temperatures regularly topping 110°F (43°C) and the emirate's car-dominated culture, there is little incentive for physical activity unless it can be made attractive—and a chance to ride where the Formula 1 gods race certainly fits the bill.

The Yas Marina Circuit is fast and challenging, dominated by its three-quarter-mile-long (1.2 km) straightaway between turns five and six—the longest straightaway on any Formula 1 track—where dramatic overtaking moves play out at speeds of more than 200 miles an hour (320 km/h). You won't have anything like the same lateral loads on your bike, but it can be fun to imagine.

Cycling here is free, although you'll need to register in advance and check the schedule, which varies throughout the year. If you don't have a bicycle, rentals are available at the track. To keep things safe and reduce the chance of collisions, walkers and runners do their laps in a clockwise direction, while cyclists ride counterclockwise. The Formula 1 lap record is 1:26, set by Max Verstappen in 2021. Good luck trying to break it.

OPPOSITE: Embrace a different kind of cycling challenge at the Yas Marina Circuit.

THE TOUR OF THE DRAGON

Be cheered on by royalty as you traverse the remote Himalayan mountain kingdom of Bhutan in this spectacular—and challenging—one-day mountain bike race.

DISTANCE: 158 miles (254 km)   SURFACE: Mixed; mainly unpaved   LENGTH OF TRIP: 3 to 4 days
WHEN TO GO: September through November   DIFFICULTY: Challenging

Bhutan's Tour of the Dragon is said to be the world's toughest one-day mountain bike race, and it's hard to disagree. It's 158 miles (254 km) of high adventure across the remote Himalayan mountain kingdom traditionally known by the more colorful name Land of the Thunder Dragon.

Starting by lamplight at 2 a.m. in the central town of Bumthang and finishing some 12 to 15 hours later in the kingdom's capital, Thimphu, the race winds its way through the heart of Bhutan's towering mountains, crosses four lofty passes, and involves more than 15,000 feet (4,570 m) of elevation gain in all. It's far longer and higher than the Tour de France, with more climbing on much, much rougher roads. Fewer than half the starters finish within the time limit.

The race is the brainchild of His Royal Highness Prince Jigyel Wangchuck, half brother to the king and a mountain bike enthusiast, who dreamed up, rode in, and completed the inaugural event in 2010 and continues to take a hands-on interest in the race, mingling with competitors beforehand, following the field by car, and occasionally getting on his bike and pedaling alongside tiring riders to offer support and encouragement. The race, the cycling, and His Highness's cheerful humanity all factor into Bhutan's famous "gross domestic happiness" quotient: a genuine index by which this remarkable country measures its success and prosperity. As HRH Prince Jigyel puts it: How

OPPOSITE: A biker speeds by a stupa, one of many dome-shaped Buddhist shrines on the race route.

PAGES 354-55: Competitors race amid the clouds on a dirt highway in the mountains of Bhutan.

can a nation be happy if people don't play sports?

As you pedal out of Bumthang by the glow of your headlamp, following a river upstream and into the hills toward your first pass of the day, you could be forgiven for thinking that this is an odd way to seek happiness. But know this: For the next 15 hours or so, you'll be living life to the fullest.

If the road is unnerving in the predawn darkness, it's a revelation by daylight: narrow, twisting, steep, prone to landslides, clinging to the sides of cliffs, and offering stunning mountain views at every bend. It crawls over passes, plunges into deep forested valleys, and passes rural villages, Buddhist shrines (stupas), colorful arrays of flags fluttering in the breeze, and those dramatic fortress monasteries, such as the imposing 16th-century Trongsa Dzong, built on a rocky spur and dominating the countryside.

The four mountain passes are your waypoints: Kiki (9,416 feet/2,870 meters), then Yotong (11,266 feet/3,434 meters), Pele (11,253 feet/3,430 meters), and finally the harrowing switchbacks up Dochu

CYCLING THROUGH HISTORY

In a market-driven world, Bhutan is unique in taking happiness into consideration. Gross domestic happiness (GDH) is a term coined in 1972 by King Jigme Wangchuck, who declared it to be more important than gross domestic product. Psychological well-being, health, education, time use, cultural diversity, good governance, community vitality, ecological resilience, and living standards all go into calculating the nation's GDH. Unsurprisingly for the bicycle-mad mountain kingdom, the ability to get out regularly on your bike scores quite highly.

ABOVE: Communities along the route offer support and encouragement to riders throughout the race.

OPPOSITE: Paro Taktsang (Tiger's Nest) Monastery, a sacred Vajrayana Himalayan Buddhist site, clings to the cliffside of the Paro Valley in Bhutan.

(10,334 feet/3,150 meters), the pass that proves to be the breaking point for many riders. Once over Dochu Pass, it's a long descent into Thimphu and the town square, where the Tour of the Dragon finishes.

The race is held during the first week of September, when the air is cooler and fresher. Open to all, it draws the bold and brave from across the globe. If you're not quite up to tackling the full Tour of the Dragon, there is a much shorter 37-mile (60 km) version called Dragon's Fury. While there's considerable cachet in completing the Tour of the Dragon within the allotted time limit, the spectacular mountain scenery and the people and vibrant Buddhist culture of Bhutan itself make this a ride also worth doing at a more leisurely pace. You'll need outfitters to help you organize your ride, as there is no unrestricted tourism here. Visitor numbers are strictly limited. They find it's better for the gross domestic happiness index.

LAKE DUNSTAN TRAIL

Explore one of New Zealand's most incredible gorges on a jaw-dropping cantilevered bike path bolted onto the rock face.

DISTANCE: 34 miles (55 km)   **SURFACE:** Crushed stone, platforms bolted onto cliff faces
LENGTH OF TRIP: 1 day   **WHEN TO GO:** Spring or autumn   **DIFFICULTY:** Easy to moderate

A showstopping feat of engineering, the Lake Dunstan Trail is arguably one of the world's most breathtaking bicycle paths. Starting off in the old Central Otago goldfields, it runs through one of New Zealand's finest wine-producing regions and along the cliff faces of the impressive Cromwell Gorge, rolling along a series of cantilevered boardwalks bolted into the rock while offering stunning views and an exhilarating sense of adventure.

If you feel like a bit of a prelude, you can start the ride at Smith's Way and pedal the 10 miles (16 km) or so along the shores of Lake Dunstan to the historic town of Cromwell, the site of a gold rush in 1862. Fertile soils and a lovely climate made this the fruit bowl of New Zealand, with long-term riches now coming from orchards and vineyards and olive groves.

The ride itself officially starts in the heritage area of Cromwell and rolls out along an arm of Lake Dunstan, through the Bannockburn wine country. The trail winds its way past the Carrick Winery, which is open for wine tasting and meals. Once past Cornish Point, the landscape takes a dramatic turn as you head into the gorge. Here you encounter your first sections of the boardwalks attached to the cliff faces. They are narrow and exposed and take a bit of nerve to ride, but the views are stunning.

OPPOSITE: Young bikers set off around Lake Dunstan during fall.

PAGES 360–61: A cantilevered bridge steers the Lake Dunstan Trail around the water near Cromwell.

At Cairnmuir Gully you drop down to lake level, where you can get a coffee at a remarkable little café on a floating pontoon called, appropriately enough, Coffee Afloat. The café also serves scones and burgers and adds a quirky bit of civilization to what is otherwise a remote stretch of gorge.

What follows is the trickiest and most challenging section: Climbing out of Cairnmuir Gully on a series of switchbacks known as the Cairnmuir Ladder takes you to the highest point on the trail, some 425 feet (130 m) above the lake.

The next remarkable piece of engineering is the 300-foot-long (91 m) Hugo suspension bridge, soaring nearly 100 feet (30 m) above the floor of the gorge. A walkable—if steep—alternative is available. Another stunning stretch of boardwalk follows—some of the trickiest to build along the entire the route—before you reach Halfway Hut viewpoint. This is something of a misnomer, for by now you are well over halfway through the ride. From here it is a fairly straightforward run to the finish in the heritage district in Clyde, another historic gold rush town. You can link up here with the western end of the lovely Otago Central Rail Trail.

ALTERNATE ROUTE

Continue your adventure on the Otago Central Rail Trail, New Zealand's first rails-to-trails cycle path, opened in 2000. The original train line, which operated between 1879 and 1990, was considered one of the world's great rail journeys, and the 94-mile-long (151 km) gravel cycling path that replaced it has become one of the country's best loved trails.

OVALAU

Pedal in paradise around one of Fiji's quietest, prettiest, most laid-back islands.

DISTANCE: **33 miles (53 km)**   SURFACE: **Gravel**   LENGTH OF TRIP: **1 day**
WHEN TO GO: **Anytime (it's Fiji)**   DIFFICULTY: **Easy to moderate**

Back in the bad old days of the early 19th century, Levuka had a colorful reputation of being one of the wickedest ports in the South Pacific, a honeypot for hard-drinking, two-fisted whalers, traders, and South Seas adventurers, renowned for its grog shops and brothels. The town's wide-open days came to an end in 1874, when the local king, Seru Cakobau, ceded the islands to Queen Victoria to repay some debts, and Levuka, as the new colony's capital, was obliged to clean up its act.

A few years later when the colonial administration shifted to Suva, on the neighboring island of Viti Levu, Levuka slipped into a long and genteel decline. Jump forward nearly 150 years and Levuka is one of the best preserved of the historic South Seas ports, with its wooden false-front buildings along Beach Street, the old Royal Hotel (dating from 1904 and the oldest hotel in the South Pacific), and the Ovalau Club, which looks like something out of a W. Somerset Maugham novel—a step back in time.

To add to the sense of old-style tropical adventure, rent a bicycle and ride the 33-mile (53 km) loop road around this unspoiled island. The route follows a quiet gravel road that takes you on a hilly ride through lush rainforests, coconut groves, and a scattering of small outlying villages, and along secluded beaches, before returning you to this delightfully unspoiled town. The slow pace and intimacy of bicycling through the landscape recalls a gentler age of travel. Finish off the day's adventure with a drink at the Ovalau Club and maybe a game of billiards on its century-old table.

OPPOSITE: Loop the island on this relaxing route circumnavigating the island of Ovalau.

NULLARBOR PLAIN

Haunting desolation and the world's longest straightaway along Australia's most iconic outback highway

DISTANCE: 750 miles (1,207 km)   **SURFACE: Paved**   **LENGTH OF TRIP: 7 to 10 days**
WHEN TO GO: October through November   **DIFFICULTY: Challenging**

"A hideous anomaly, a blot on the face of Nature, the sort of place one gets into in bad dreams . . ." So wrote the explorer Edward John Eyre of Australia's vast, waterless Nullarbor Plain after becoming, on his third attempt, the first European to cross it in 1841. He and his Aboriginal guide, Wylie, had only barely survived the journey, after being nearly dead with thirst and hunger and literally crawling the last few miles.

These days crossing the Nullarbor is far easier and one of Australia's most iconic road trips along the eerily desolate Eyre Highway. Making the trip to this 100,000-square-mile (258,999 sq km) expanse of arid limestone plain has become something of an Australian right of passage. And there is no better way to do it than on a bicycle.

While many people regard "crossing the Nullarbor" to mean the entire journey from Perth to Adelaide (1,674 miles/2,694 kilometers), technically speaking the Nullarbor begins at the edge of the lonely old gold mining town of Norseman, about 450 miles (725 km) east of Perth. There are no towns and very limited resources ahead for the next 750 miles (1,205 km), only a lonely archipelago of oasis-like roadhouses with long, long, long stretches of emptiness in between.

"Nullarbor" is Latin and comes from a linking of *null* and *arbor,* meaning "no trees." It was given the name by the surveyor Edmund Delisser, who crossed it in 1865. While it's an apt description for the vast majority of the

OPPOSITE: The incredible cliffs along the Great Australian Bight, a large, open bay that protects a calving area for southern right whales

PAGES 366-67: Wildlife encounters can take on numerous forms while cycling the Eyre Highway.

plain, the portion crossed by the highway is in fact lightly wooded much of the way.

And the ride across the Nullarbor is not dull. The slow pace of a bicycle is perfect for picking up the details one misses when hurtling along in a car. There's beautiful salmon gums, bluebush and mulga scrub, wildflowers, raucous birds, and opportunities to encounter kangaroos, emus, wombats, and herds of wild camels.

The first stop after leaving Norseman is the Balladonia Roadhouse, some 118 miles (190 km) distant. It was out here in 1979 that the NASA space station Skylab famously crashed to Earth. A museum at Balladonia displays bits of the space station and has exhibits about Aboriginal heritage.

It's just over 100 miles (161 km) to the next little oasis on the plain, Caiguna Roadhouse. Most of the way, you'll be pedaling on the world's longest dead-straight stretch of road—91 miles (146 km) without so much as a kink. You'll see a couple of iconic road signs worth a photo stop: one announcing the world's longest straightaway and a triptych of signs warning motorists to beware of wildlife.

Cocklebiddy, Madura, Mundrabilla, Eucla—the

ALTERNATE ROUTE

As you pedal across the Nullarbor, you can play the world's longest golf course, an 848-mile (1,365 km) par 72 that stretches from the rollicking Old West gold mining town of Kalgoorlie to the lonely tuna fishing port of Ceduna, in South Australia. If you want to start from the first hole, begin your ride in Kalgoorlie, 116 miles (187 km) farther west, instead of in Norseman.

ABOVE: **Vibrant wild grevillea along the Eyre Highway on the Nullarbor Plain**

OPPOSITE: **Chris Anderson circumnavigated Australia by bicycle to raise awareness and funds for Beyond Blue, an organization that promotes mental health awareness.**

roadhouses pass one after the other, interspersed with long stretches of arid scrub, "the great Australian loneliness," as 1930s travel writer Ernestine Hill described it. Eucla is one of the nicest oases along the route, with its historic telegraph station and a haunting expanse of dunes. Eight miles (12.9 km) past Eucla, you cross the South Australian border at the Border Village Roadhouse. East of here, the highway runs along the top of the Bunda Cliffs—a 124-mile-long (200 km) stretch of banded cliffs overlooking the Great Australian Bight, a vast stretch of the Southern Ocean. This is the longest line of sea cliffs in the world. The sense of timelessness and remoteness as you stand along their edge is worth the ride all on its own. Nullarbor, Nundroo, and Penong roadhouses await before you finally roll into Ceduna, a lonely tuna-fishing port that feels like Manhattan after the Eyre Highway. You're still 475 miles (765 km) from the nearest city (Adelaide), but you've done it. You've crossed the Nullarbor Plain.

ALPS 2 OCEAN CYCLE TRAIL

A cinematic ride through a cavalcade of the South Island's most beautiful landscapes along New Zealand's most popular long-distance cycle route

DISTANCE: 190 miles (306 km)   **SURFACE:** Varied; gravel, paved roads, paths   **LENGTH OF TRIP:** 4 to 6 days
WHEN TO GO: November through March   **DIFFICULTY:** Easy to moderate

The Alps 2 Ocean (A2O) Cycle Trail is one of New Zealand's most iconic bicycle routes and its longest continuous bike trail as well, stretching some 190 miles (306 km) from the base of New Zealand's highest mountain, the majestic 12,316-foot (3,754 m) Aoraki (aka Mount Cook), before ending at the Victorian coastal town of Oamaru. Along the way, the trail passes through some of the loveliest scenery in New Zealand's South Island. Although the trail can be ridden in either direction, most thru-riders start in the mountains and ride to the sea—it's mainly downhill, and you have the prevailing winds with you.

The adventure of riding A2O begins right away. Accessing the ultimate starting point on the trail, nestled at the base of Aoraki, means getting a short (six-minute) helicopter flight from the Mount Cook Airport across the Tasman River to a spot known as Rotten Tommy and following a gravel track along the braided Tasman delta down to the shores of Lake Pukaki.

The flight itself offers stunning views of the snowcapped peak and the Southern Alps, and the helicopters are equipped to carry up to five bicycles and their riders at a time. If you would rather save the money and skip the helicopter flight, you can begin the ride at alternative—and also scenic—starting points, either at the lower end of Lake Pukaki or from Lake Tekapo, and follow the hydroelectric

PHOTO OP

Alps 2 Ocean is the longest route of "the Journeys," a collection of 23 predominantly off-road trails. Three of the routes— Hauraki Rail Trail, Alps 2 Ocean, and Otago Central Rail Trail—were named in the top 30 of the most Instagrammed trails in the world.

OPPOSITE: Plan to stop at a local winery while cycling the Alps 2 Ocean Cycle Trail.

PAGES 372-73: You can't miss the fields of limestone known as Elephant Rocks on the lower valley portion of the trail.

canal south to the lower end of Lake Pukaki. All these alternate beginnings come together by the time the trail passes through the town of Twizel, some 35 miles (56 km) from whichever starting point you choose.

Twizel was built in the late 1960s for workers constructing the giant Waitaki hydroelectric system and is now a hub for backcountry adventures. The luminous blue glacial lakes, dams, and canals of the hydroelectric scheme are a kind of coda for much of the A2O trail as it winds its way down through the mountains toward the sea.

The 23-mile (37 km) stretch from Twizel to Lake Ohau is one of the highlights, following quiet country roads and the banks of another of the hydroelectric scheme's canals. From Lake Ohau the trail veers southeasterly toward the Waitaki Valley. After a brief bit of climbing, the trail continues its long, winding downward trek toward the sea through some of New Zealand's loveliest wine districts. It's a generally easy ride, on gravel tracks or quiet roads, and finishes with a breezy downhill glide into Oamaru, famous for its public gardens and its historic district built of local limestone.

REST STOP

Take time out of the saddle to explore the Waitaki wine region. Vines were first planted here in 2001, with pioneering vintners taking advantage of the valley's limestone-based soils and microclimate to produce award-winning cool-weather varieties. About a dozen boutique labels are found in the valley, and their wines can be paired nicely in local restaurants with seafood from the nearby fishing village of Moeraki.

FORGOTTEN WORLD HIGHWAY

Plunge into a gorge that time forgot along New Zealand's oldest heritage trail.

DISTANCE: **114 miles (183 km)**   SURFACE: **Mainly paved**   LENGTH OF TRIP: **1 to 2 days**
WHEN TO GO: **Summer through autumn**   DIFFICULTY: **Challenging**

Step back in time on a rustic backroad that follows the line of colonial 19th-century bridle paths through the mountains and gorges of one of New Zealand's most remote districts on its oldest heritage trail.

Starting in Taumarunui, the Forgotten World Highway—its official, less romantic, name is State Highway 43—rolls past a lovely lavender farm and along the Whanganui River for 18 miles (29 km) or so before you pedal up and over Paparata Saddle, then plunge down into Tangarakau Gorge.

Here the road turns to gravel for the next eight miles (12.9 km) as it winds its way through this ancient *Jurassic Park*–like gorge, with its big ferns, waterfalls, and jagged cliffs. Passing through the 600-foot-long (183 m) single-lane Moki Tunnel, known as the Hobbit's Hole, adds to the sense of adventure. Another climb up and over Tahora Saddle brings you to the quirky town of Whangamomona, settled in 1895 by a motley lot of independent-minded pioneers.

From Whangamomona the Forgotten World route leaves State Highway 43 and follows Junction Road through the remote backcountry. Two more mountain passes—"saddles" in the local vernacular—await as you make your way toward the coast, together with another tunnel and a historic suspension bridge spanning the Waitara River. The ride ends gloriously, with a spin along the stunning New Plymouth Coastal Walkway, an eight-mile-long (13 km) shared footpath that leads you into the pretty coastal town of New Plymouth.

OPPOSITE: **The Maramataha suspension bridge high above the tree line on the Timber Trail in Pureora Forest Park**

KUNUNURRA TO DERBY, WESTERN AUSTRALIA, AUSTRALIA

GIBB RIVER ROAD

Crocodile Dundee–like adventure—complete with actual crocodiles—in Australia's famously rugged and remote Kimberley region

DISTANCE: **410 miles (660 km)**   SURFACE: **Gravel, a few paved sections**   LENGTH OF TRIP: **7 to 14 days**
WHEN TO GO: **May through October (dry season)**   DIFFICULTY: **Challenging**

Originally built as a stock route during the 1960s to link the region's remote cattle stations with the deep-water ports of Derby and Wyndham, the Gibb River Road crosses an ancient landscape of gorges, rocky crags, waterfalls, and prehistoric rivers where crocodiles await the unwary. Set in Australia's legendary Kimberley region, in the far northwest of the continent, it is a stunning expedition of a ride through one of the most beautiful and most remote sections of the outback.

Start the journey at Kununurra, a leafy green oasis town in the far east of the Kimberley that was built on the back of an ambitious land-taming project of the early 1960s in which the floodwaters of the Ord River were dammed to form Lake Argyle and create a fertile pocket of farmland in the desert. The view from Kelly's Knob, a rocky promontory above the town, illustrates the peculiar oasis-like feel of the town, an island of green in a vast expanse of red-rock scrub.

From Kununurra, follow the paved Great Northern Highway west for about 25 miles (40 km) until you to come to the turnoff for Gibb River Road on your right, where the gravel adventure begins. How rough the road is depends on how much rain fell during the wet season. The same holds true for the river crossings—there are no bridges out here. Rivers have to be forded. Much caution is required. The broadest of these rivers, the Pentecost, might be only knee-deep during the dry season, but there are crocodiles present. Big ones. Many cyclists wait for a passing truck or 4WD and cadge a lift if they

OPPOSITE: Cyclists cross the Pentecost River in Kimberley, Western Australia, on the Gibb River Road.

PAGES 378-79: Distinctive baobab trees near the Gibb River Road cycling route

can. And with these same scary reptiles in mind, never camp close to a river or any permanent water; about 330 feet (100 m) is usually reckoned a good distance.

But then this is all part of the adventure. There is nothing tame about the landscapes here. The road passes through or near a series of spectacular gorges, of which the best known and most accessible is Windjana Gorge, formed from a 300-million-year-old reef. Bell Gorge, often claimed to be the most beautiful, means taking an 18-mile (29 km) detour (each way) but is well worth the trip. If you were in a hurry, you wouldn't be out here.

The ride ends in Derby, its eerie-looking baobab trees adding to the primordial feel of the landscape. If you feel like rewarding yourself with a little luxury after your outback adventure, the stylish old pearling port of Broome, with its resorts and fabulous white sand strand of beach, is only another 137 miles (220 km) down the highway.

ALTERNATE ROUTE

If you're looking to get off the beaten path, try taking the turnoff onto the Kalumburu Road, about 150 miles (240 km) from Kununurra, to the spectacular Mitchell River National Park, one of Australia's most remote national parks. It's a good 100 miles (161 km) to the park boundary and then another 50 miles (80 km) or so along the challenging Mitchell Plateau Track to reach the park's campground. The Kalumburu Road continues 65 miles (105 km) to the extremely remote Aboriginal settlement of Kalumburu; remember to apply for a permit if you wish to visit.

MUNDA BIDDI TRAIL

Explore Western Australia's towering karri forests along one of the world's most remote wilderness cycle paths.

DISTANCE: 659 miles (1,060 km)   **SURFACE:** Gravel; world's longest off-road cycling trail
LENGTH OF TRIP: 2 to 3 weeks   **WHEN TO GO:** September through October   **DIFFICULTY:** Easy to moderate

The southwest corner of Western Australia is like a separate world from the rest of Australia, a hidden wonderland of beautiful river valleys and towering karri forests that has remained surprisingly and blissfully undiscovered. During the spring, spectacular displays of more than 12,000 different species of wildflowers bloom, most of them found nowhere else on Earth. And it's in this vast tract of antipodean wilderness that you find the Munda Biddi Trail—at just over 650 miles (1,046 km), reputedly the world's longest continuous off-road cycling trail.

The name Munda Biddi comes from the local Noongar Aboriginal language and means "path through the forest." Starting at Mundaring, the trail follows a network of fire tracks, bush paths, and old railway lines through forest and farmlands to the south coast. The vast majority of the Munda Biddi Trail is off-road and traffic free, and gravel or mountain bikes are the best choices. Although very much a wilderness route, the Munda Biddi Trail was designed so that each day you finish near a small bush town or at a purpose-built campsite.

From the Sculpture Park in Mundaring, the trail meanders through the magnificent jarrah forests to the wine country of the Ferguson Valley. As you amble farther south, the forests grow even more majestic. You're in the land of the giants, dwarfed by karri trees towering nearly 300 feet (90 m) above the forest floor. When you reach Pemberton, you can try climbing one of these giant trees on the pegs that were once used by foresters to access the

OPPOSITE: A kangaroo says hello at the old school building at Donnelly River Village along the Munda Biddi Trail.

PAGES 382-83: Thick trees shade a rider in a karri forest outside Northcliffe.

fire-lookout platforms. The climb to the 209-foot-high (64 m) platform on the Dave Evans Bicentennial Tree is said to be Western Australia's scariest tourist attraction. Fewer than one in five visitors hold their nerve and make it to the top. A less stressful alternative is to lay over for a day and hike the seven-mile (11.2 km) Warren River Loop Walk through the forest.

South of Pemberton the trail takes on an even wilder feel, with longer stretches between towns such as Walpole and Denmark, until at last you arrive on the coast at the remote town of Albany, and a beautiful end to the ride. Once the site of Australia's last operating whaling station, the pretty, windswept town is now a splendid place for whale-watching, with southern right and humpback whales coming into the sound to breed between May and November.

The Munda Biddi Trail can be done any time of the year, but the best season is the late-winter and early-spring months of September and October, when Western Australia's famous wildflower displays are in full swing.

REST STOP

Western Australia is a botanist's dream. More than 12,000 species of wildflowers can be found here, with more than 60 percent of them found nowhere else on Earth. Come at the right time of year—September through October—and you don't even need to leave the city to see them. Kings Park, a sprawling 1,000-acre (405 ha) tract of bushland in the heart of Perth, Western Australia's capital city, is home to hundreds of species. Cycling tours are available.

MAWSON TRAIL

Ride from the heart of Australia's most genteel capital city to the spectacular Flinders Ranges in the outback—off-road and nearly traffic free the whole way.

DISTANCE: **560 miles (901 km)**   SURFACE: **Mixed; from smooth tarmac to rough tracks**
LENGTH OF TRIP: **8 to 10 days**   WHEN TO GO: **Spring through autumn**   DIFFICULTY: **Challenging**

The city of Adelaide—known as the City of Churches—was the springboard for many an outback expedition back in Australia's colonial days. Today the elegant South Australian capital is the springboard for expedition cyclists taking on the Mawson Trail, an epic gravel biking adventure that takes you from the posh environs of North Terrace, Adelaide's premier boulevard, up into the leafy Adelaide Hills, before ending hundreds of miles away in the craggy, wild, and remote Flinders Ranges.

The Mawson Trail is named for Sir Douglas Mawson, an eminent South Australian geologist better known for his heroics as an Antarctic explorer than for his work in the Flinders Ranges. To connect with the trail from downtown Adelaide, follow the River Torrens Linear Trail, a popular commuter route that traces the River Torrens upstream toward Athelstone and the Adelaide Hills. From Athelstone a short ride along Gorge Road brings you to the southern terminus of the Mawson Trail and the start of the adventure.

How easy or hard the Mawson Trail is depends mostly on the weather. In dry conditions it's moderately challenging. In wet it morphs into a seriously tough trek. The trail meanders all over the Adelaide Hills along a network of fire tracks and dirt roads through miles of eucalyptus forest before leading you down into the beautiful Barossa Valley.

Settled by Germans in the 1840s, the Barossa is one of the world's great wine-producing regions. The valley's German heritage lives on in the traditional bakeries and old-style family-run butcher shops.

OPPOSITE: This iconic view from Razorback Lookout into Ikara–Flinders Ranges National Park is the prize at the end of a climb through the northern end of the trail.

PAGES 386-87: This old telegraph dirt road runs toward Ikara-Wilpena in South Australia's Flinders Ranges.

From the Barossa Valley the trail winds its way north across a vast expanse of wide-open farmland, through the rolling vineyards of the Clare Valley, and on to the old copper-mining boomtown of Burra, one of South Australia's best preserved Victorian-era towns.

North of Burra, the landscape opens up. Pedal through undulating farmlands, mallee scrub, and forest on gravel tracks. You're now in what's known as the Mid North of South Australia. The sky is bigger; the towns are smaller and farther apart. You can see for miles.

Not long after you leave Quorn, after a steep climb up Yarrah Vale Gorge Road, you get your first proper views of the Flinders Ranges, hazy and purplish in the distance. As you wind your way ever farther north, the scenery gets wilder and more dramatic, reaching its high point in the mountains surrounding Wilpena Pound and the panoramic views at Razorback Ridge. The final signpost in Blinman points the way to the pub. As you knock back a cold beer, the lights and bustle of Adelaide, the city where the adventure started, seem a million miles away.

ARMCHAIR RIDE

Australian Sir Douglas Mawson's monthlong solo Antarctic survival epic in 1912—when his companions perished and he was forced to travel alone through heavily crevassed ice fields to reach his base camp—is the stuff of legend. His account, *The Home of the Blizzard,* is regarded as an Antarctic classic.

MURRAY TO MOUNTAINS

Experience some of Australia's most iconic bush landscapes and historic gold rush towns along the nation's premier rails-to-trails path.

DISTANCE: 58 miles (93 km) **SURFACE:** Paved **LENGTH OF TRIP:** 1 to 3 days
WHEN TO GO: April through May, or November **DIFFICULTY:** Easy to moderate

The Murray to Mountains Rail Trail runs along the line of the old Bright Railway, through miles of sweet-scented eucalyptus forest in Wangaratta to the alpine town of Bright, with a 10-mile-long (16 km) side spur to the beautifully preserved historic town of Beechworth.

This is a ride for epicures as much as cyclists. Pedal past vineyards and world-class wineries with cellar-door tastings as you roll through Victoria's gourmet region, where small-town cafés and restaurants turn out meals with big-city sophistication.

Despite its name, the Murray to Mountains Rail Trail doesn't actually start along the Murray River. If you want to begin your ride along the Murray, you need to detour to Rutherglen, about 25 miles (40 km) northeast of the trail's official start at Wangaratta. From Rutherglen you can take a lovely six-mile (10 km) rails-to-trails path to Wahgunyah on the banks of the Murray, and while you're in the area explore the local wineries, maybe pick up a bottle of De Bortoli's the Noble One, a world-class Botrytis Sémillon dessert wine that has won more awards than any other wine in Australia.

The ride from the Rutherglen and Wahgunyah area to Wangaratta and the start of the Murray to Mountains Rail Trail is along a main road. Once you're on the trail, there's no more traffic, no steep grades to speak of, and

OPPOSITE: Vineyards line the trail near Bright in Victoria.

PAGES 390-91: A long day of riding calls for a moment of zen by the Ovens River in Porepunkah.

it's all paved. It's very civilized spinning along through the farmland, with its iconic windmills and the warbling of magpies. If you're interested in Australia's colonial history, this is Ned Kelly country, the pocket of northeast Victoria where the legendary bushranger and his gang operated and hid out during the late 1870s, assisted in no small part by some of the locals, who sympathized with his antiestablishment views and occasionally benefited from his Robin Hood–style largesse.

Seventeen miles (27 km) south of Wangaratta, near Everton Station, you come to the spur line to Beechworth. It's a 10-mile (16 km) side trip—20-mile (32 km) round trip—but well worth it. Beechworth is beautiful, the best preserved of Victoria's gold rush towns, famed for its honeyed sandstone buildings and with plenty of period pubs.

This optional side trip to Beechworth involves the only significant climb along the Murray to Mountains Rail Trail, but that also means an easy glide back to the main stem. Another 17 miles (27 km) brings you to Myrtleford, a lovely little town with plenty of cafés and local wineries. The final stretch from here to Bright is especially scenic as you come into the alpine country. In autumn the high country towns of Bright and Beechworth both put on beautiful displays of fall foliages. If you still have a bit of extra energy, the four-mile (6 km) side trip to the quaint old gold mining town of Wandiligong is well worth it.

RIDES BY COUNTRY

ARGENTINA
Ruta de los Siete
    Lagos 150

AUSTRALIA
Gibb River Road 376
Mawson Trail 384
Munda Biddi Trail 380
Murray to Mountains 388
Nullarbor Plain 364

AUSTRIA
Danube Cycle Path . . . 174
Lake Constance Cycle
    Path 188

BHUTAN
The Tour of the
    Dragon 352

BOLIVIA
La Carretera de los
    Yungas 124
Salar de Uyuni 158

CAMBODIA
Ancient Angkor 326

CANADA
Cabot Trail 106
The Great Divide 88
Kettle Valley Rail Trail . 48
Mountain Hero 126
Underground Railroad
    Route 30
Véloroute des
    Bleuets 118

CHILE
Carretera Austral 146

CHINA
Qinghai Lake 316

COSTA RICA
La Ruta de los
    Conquistadores . . . 160

CUBA
La Farola 72

DENMARK
Danish North Coast
    Bicycle Route 47 . . . 180

ECUADOR
Trans Ecuador MTB
    Route 164

ENGLAND
Cantii Way 242
Dunwich Dynamo
    Route 212
Fred Whitton
    Challenge 280
King Alfred's Way 168
South Downs Way 228
Way of the Roses 292

FIJI
Ovalau 362

FRANCE
El Camino
    de Santiago 240
Canal du Midi 248

Col du Tourmalet 272
Corsican Coast. 290
Île de Ré. 296
La Vélodyssée 192
Loire à Vélo. 234
Mont Ventoux. 202
Paris-Brest-Paris. 182
Paris-Roubaix 260
Tour de Mont
    Aigoual. 222

GERMANY
Berlin Wall Trail 298
Danube Cycle Path. . . 174
Lake Constance
    Cycle Path 188
Romantic Road 254
Southern Black Forest
    Cycle Route. 284

ICELAND
The Ring Road. 208

INDIA
Manali-Leh
    Highway. 342

IRELAND
Ring of Kerry 258

ITALY
Ciclabile delle
    Dolomiti 172

Gavia-Mortirolo
    Loop 266
L'Eroica. 200

JAPAN
Shimanami Kaido 324

KYRGYZSTAN
Pamir Highway. 346

MEXICO
The Baja Divide 58

NETHERLANDS
Rhine Cycle
    Route. 214

NEW ZEALAND
Alps 2 Ocean Cycle
    Trail 370
Forgotten World
    Highway 374
Lake Dunstan Trail. . . . 358

NORWAY
Birkebeinerrittet. 232
Rallarvegen 278

PERU
Huascarán Circuit 152

RWANDA
Congo-Nile Trail 308

SCOTLAND
Applecross Loop 252

SLOVENIA
West Loop 286

SOUTH AFRICA
Cape of Good
    Hope. 314
Swartberg Pass 304

SOUTH KOREA
4 Rivers Path. 318

SPAIN
El Camino
    de Santiago. 240
Cap de Formentor . . . 270
Costa Brava Loop 220

SWITZERLAND
Lake Constance
    Cycle Path 188
Rhine Cycle Route . . . 214

TAIWAN
Sun Moon Lake 330

TAJIKISTAN
Pamir Highway. 346

THAILAND
Mae Hong Son Loop . 332

UNITED ARAB EMIRATES
Yas Marina Circuit 350

UNITED STATES
ALASKA
Denali Park Road 24

CALIFORNIA
The Baja Divide 58
Kings Canyon 40
Mount Tam 132

COLORADO
Colorado Trail 138

HAWAII
Mauna Kea 112

IDAHO
Trail of the Coeur
    d'Alenes 86

IOWA
RAGBRAI 76

MAINE
Carriage Roads 12

MARYLAND
Chesapeake & Ohio
    Canal Towpath 54
Great Allegheny
    Passage 18

MICHIGAN
Old Mission Peninsula
    Trail 74

MISSISSIPPI
Natchez Trace
    Parkway 140

MISSOURI
The Katy Trail 134

MONTANA
Going-to-the-Sun
    Road 100

MULTISTATE
The Great Divide 88
TransAmerica Trail 66
Underground Railroad
    Route 30

NEW YORK
Empire State Trail 52

NORTH CAROLINA
Blue Ridge Parkway . . . 94

OREGON
Banks-Vernonia State
    Trail 16
Crater Lake Scenic
    Rim Drive 82
Tour de Fronds 28

PENNSYLVANIA
Great Allegheny
    Passage 18

SOUTH DAKOTA
George S. Mickelson
    Trail 36

TENNESSEE
Natchez Trace
    Parkway 140

UTAH
Wasatch Crest Trail 64
White Rim Trail 120
The Whole Enchilada . 42

VIRGINIA
Blue Ridge Parkway . . . 94
New River Trail 60

WASHINGTON
San Juan Islands 98

WASHINGTON, D.C.
Chesapeake & Ohio
    Canal Towpath 54

WEST VIRGINIA
Greenbrier River Trail .110

VIETNAM
Ho Chi Minh
    Highway 338

WALES
Lôn Las Cymru 194

ACKNOWLEDGMENTS

So many cyclists from all parts of the globe and with all different styles and disciplines of riding provided input, suggestions, practical advice, and stories from the road that helped make up this list of 100 bike rides of a lifetime. They include David Cain, Matthew Sowter, Steven Smith, Jay Rawlins, Alex Strickland, Adam Ruck, India Landy, Timo Langerwerf, Erick Cedeno, Nichola Roberts, Susan Lash, Lionel Birnie, David Clarke, Mark McKay, Andrew Richman, Marc Silver, Richard Monastersky, Ian Lloyd, David Rodriguez, Dan Craven, Sam Jones, Sophie Gordon, Stefan Amato, Bill Manning, Saskia Marlow, Tricia Dwyer, Francesca Fumagalli, Rory Doyle, Mauro Tarani, Lexi Dowdall, Leah Day, and Mark Shotter.

Thank you, too, to the team at National Geographic: editorial director Lisa Thomas, senior editor Allyson Johnson, project editor Ashley Leath, art director Nicole Miller Roberts, designer Kay Hankins, senior photo editor Jill Foley, photo editor Charlie Borst, senior production editor Michael O'Connor, and production editor Becca Saltzman.

ILLUSTRATIONS CREDITS

Cover, kovop/Shutterstock; back cover, Sterling Lorence; 2-3, Sterling Lorence; 4-5, Patrick Escudero/hemis/Alamy Stock Photo; 7, Harry How/Getty Images; 9, Cass Gilbert; 10-1, Logan Watts; 13, Tim Laman/NG Image Collection; 14-5, Richard Nieves/Shutterstock; 17, Andrea Johnson Photography/Travel Portland; 19 and 20-1, Doug Riegner, GAP Conservancy; 22, William Wotring/Alamy Stock Photo; 23, Edwin Remsberg/VWPics via AP Images; 25, Joe Stock/Design Pics/Alamy Stock Photo; 26-7, Cultura RM Exclusive/Seth K. Hughes/Getty Images; 29, George Ostertag/Alamy Stock Photo; 31 and 32, Dennis Coello; 34, Jeffrey Isaac Greenberg 16+/Alamy Stock Photo; 35-9 Dennis Coello; 41, Ian Stout/Cavan Images; 43, Scott Markewitz; 44-5, Paris Gore; 46 and 47, Sterling Lorence; 49, Chuck Haney; 50-1, Frank Heuer/laif/Redux; 53, Robert K. Chin/Alamy Stock Photo; 55, Skip Brown/NG Image Collection; 56-7, Sam Kittner/NG Image Collection; 59, Cass Gilbert; 61, Courtesy Virginia State Parks; 62-3, Edwin Remsberg/VWPics via AP Images; 65, Scott Markewitz; 67-71, Chris Hytha; 73, Alexandre ROSA/Alamy Stock Photo; 75, Chuck Haney; 77 and 78-9, Dennis Coello; 80, AP Photo/Charlie Neibergall; 81, Lane Turner/The Boston Globe via Getty Images; 83, Dennis Coello; 84-5, Larry Geddis/Alamy; 87, Universal Images Group via Getty Images; 89, Larry Clouse/Cal Sport Media via ZUMA Wire/AP Images; 90-1, Spring Images/Alamy Stock Photo; 92, Images By T.O.K./Alamy Stock Photo; 93, Larry Clouse/Cal Sport Media via ZUMA Wire/AP Images; 95, Harrison Shull/Cavan Images; 96-7, Dennis Coello; 99, Spring Images/Alamy Stock Photo; 101, AP Photo/Beth J. Harpaz; 102-3, Chuck Haney; 104, Chuck Haney/DanitaDelimont/Alamy Stock Photo; 105, Shawna Kozel/Cavan Images; 107, Michael Dwyer/Alamy Stock Photo; 108-9, Stanislas Fautre/Figarophoto/Redux; 111, Skip Brown/NG Image Collection; 113, Michael Runkel/robertharding; 114-7, Jonathan Rawle; 119, Christian Ouellet/Adobe Stock; 121, Paul Jeurissen; 122-3, Doug Pensinger/Getty Images; 125, Phil Clarke Hill/In Pictures/Corbis via Getty Images; 127, Ryan Creary/All Canada Photos/Alamy Stock Photo; 128-9, Peter Wojnar; 130, Ryan Creary/All Canada Photos/Alamy Stock Photo; 131, Stephen G. St. John; 133, Stephen Saks Photography/Alamy Stock Photo; 135 and 136-7, Dennis Coello; 139, Scott Markewitz; 141-4, Dennis Coello; 145, Bill O'Leary/The Washington Post via Getty Images; 147, Harri Jarvelainen Photography/Getty Images; 148-9 and 151, Pawel Opaska/Alamy Stock Photo; 153, Saro17/Getty Images; 154-5, Ryan Wilson; 156, Bert de Ruiter/Alamy Stock Photo; 157, Heiko Meyer/laif/Redux; 159, Paul Jeurissen; 161, Ezra Shaw/Getty Images; 162-3, Ezra Shaw/Getty Images; 165, Cass Gilbert; 166-7, Jon Sparks/Alamy Stock Photo; 169 and 170-1, Robert Spanring/Cycling UK; 173, Atelier Knox/Alamy Stock Photo; 175, zeeman/Alamy Stock Photo; 176-7, Martin Zwick/Getty Images; 178, Clemens Zahn/laif/Redux Pictures; 179, Armaroli Stefano/Alamy Stock Photo; 181, Daniel Villadsen/VisitNorthesealand; 183, Sueddeutsche Zeitung Photo/Alamy Stock Photo; 184-5, Wig Worland/Cavan Images; 186 and 187, Christophe Calais/Corbis via Getty Images; 189, Karl-Josef Hildenbrand/picture alliance via Getty Images; 190-1, Ernst Wrba/mauritius Images GmbH/Alamy Stock Photo; 193, Franck Guiziou/hemis/Alamy Stock Photo; 195, Julian Elliott Photography/Alamy Stock Photo; 196-7, Andrew Bain/Alamy Stock Photo; 198, Lucas Vallecillos/VWPics/Redux Pictures; 199, James Brooks/Alamy Stock Photo;

ABOUT THE AUTHOR

A regular contributor to *National Geographic* for more than 25 years, **Roff Smith** got his first byline in the magazine for a three-part series on his solo 10,000-mile (16,093 km) bicycle odyssey through the Australian bush. In the years since, he has cycled all over the globe, on every continent, including Antarctica, where, in a lighthearted moment while on a *National Geographic* assignment at the South Pole, he pedaled "round the world" in less than 10 seconds. He has contributed to numerous cycling magazines and edited two books on frame-building, and he is a London City & Guilds–qualified bicycle mechanic. His fine-art cycling photography project undertaken during lockdown in Sussex, titled Travels at Home, received widespread international coverage by the *New York Times*, the *Guardian,* and the BBC.

Since 1888, the National Geographic Society has funded more than 14,000 research, conservation, education, and storytelling projects around the world. National Geographic Partners distributes a portion of the funds it receives from your purchase to National Geographic Society to support programs including the conservation of animals and their habitats.

Get closer to National Geographic Explorers and photographers, and connect with our global community. Join us today at nationalgeographic.org/joinus

For rights or permissions inquiries, please contact National Geographic Books Subsidiary Rights: bookrights@natgeo.com

Library of Congress Cataloging-in-Publication Data Names: Smith, Roff Martin author.
Title: 100 bike rides of a lifetime : the world's ultimate cycling experiences / Roff Smith.
Other titles: One hundred bike rides of a lifetime
Description: Washington, DC : National Geographic, [2023] I Summary:
"This inspiring illustrated guide reveals the ultimate bucket-list destinations for cyclists"—Provided by publisher.
Identifiers: LCCN 2022059102 I ISBN 9781426222658 (hardcover)
Subjects: LCSH: Bicycle touring—Guidebooks.
Classification: LCC GV1044 .S65 2023 I DDC 910.4—dc23/eng/20230109
LC record available at https://lccn.loc.gov/202205910

ISBN: 978-1-4262-2265-8

Printed in Hong Kong

23/PPHK/1

The information in this book has been carefully checked and to the best of our knowledge is accurate. However, details are subject to change, and the publisher cannot be responsible for such changes, or for errors or omissions. Assessments of sites, hotels, and restaurants are based on the author's subjective opinions, which do not necessarily reflect the publisher's opinion.

I MORE ADVENTURES TO EXPLORE

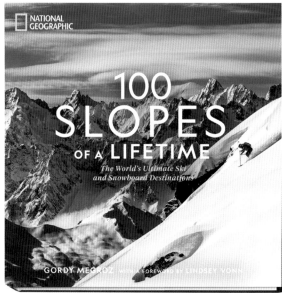